Extra muros / intra muros:

A Collaborative Exhibition
of Rare Books and Special Collections
at the University of Toronto

THE THOMAS FISHER RARE BOOK LIBRARY, UNIVERSITY OF TORONTO

September 25–December 22, 2006

Catalogue by: Jonathan Bengtson, Robert C. Brandeis, Pearce J. Carefoote, Linda Corman, Robert Doran, S.J., Gabrielle Earnshaw, James Farge, C.S.B., Alison Girling, Jack Howard, Hana Kim, Marie Korey, Richard Landon, Noel McFerran, Kathleen McMorrow, Yannick Portebois, Stephen Qiao, Sunhee Ro, Dean Seeman, Lisa Sherlock, Arthur Smith, Carmen Königsreuther Socknat, Dorothy E. Speirs, Kimberley Yates, Lorna Young, Gabbi Zaldin

General editors: Marie Korey, Pearce J. Carefoote, and Barry Walfish
Exhibition installed by: Linda Joy
Digital photography by: Jim Ingram and Bogda Mickiewicz
Cover art by: A. Scott Carter, from the Thomas Fisher Rare Book Library
Catalogue designed by: Stan Bevington
Catalogue printed and bound by: Coach House Press & University of Toronto Press

LIBRARY AND ARCHIVES CANADA CATALOGUING IN PUBLICATION

Extra muros, intra muros : a collaborative exhibition of rare books
and special collections at the University of Toronto.

Includes bibliographical references.
Catalogue of an exhibition held at the Thomas Fisher Rare Book Library,
Sept. 25-Dec. 22, 2006. Edited by Pearce J. Carefoote, Marie Korey, and Barry Walfish.
ISBN 0-7727-6060-8

1. Rare books—Exhibitions.
2. University of Toronto. Library—Exhibitions.
    I. Korey, Marie Elena
    II. Walfish, Barry Dov, 1947-
    III. Carefoote, Pearce J., 1961-
    IV. Thomas Fisher Rare Book Library
    V. Title.
Z1029.E98 2006   011'.4409713541   c2006-904066-4

Contents

Introduction

Within the walls of the Thomas Fisher Rare Book Library, there are roughly 700,000 books and many large collections of literary and historical manuscripts, including the University of Toronto Archives. It is the largest and most diverse research resource of its kind in Canada. However, without those walls, but within the University of Toronto, there are a dozen other important Special Collections departments whose resources are well known to the specialist scholars who use them, but are not, perhaps, as visible to the general university community and the citizens of Toronto. This is the first time we have attempted a joint, collaborative exhibition to display in one venue a selection of the treasures throughout the whole university.

This exhibition has been coordinated, and the catalogue has been edited, by P.J. Carefoote of the Fisher Library and Marie Korey, the Librarian of the Robertson Davies Library at Massey College, with the editorial assistance of Philip Oldfield and Barry Walfish, and, as always, the exhibition design and layout skills of Linda Joy. The catalogue has twenty-five authors, whose individual contributions are indicated by their initials. Anna U of the Cheng Yu Tung East Asian Library and Sharon Larade of the United Church of Canada/Victoria University Archives assisted in the planning stages. Four institutions, Knox College, University College, Hart House, and the Ontario Institute for Studies in Education, are represented by items which are on deposit in the Fisher Library. The Royal Ontario Museum, although it has not been part of the University of Toronto since 1968, is part of the exhibition because its library holdings are in the union catalogue and are important resources for university research. Financial support for the catalogue has come from four participating institutions: the Quadrangle Society of Massey College, the Friends of the John M. Kelly Library at St. Michael's College, the Friends of the Victoria University Library, and the Friends of Trinity College Library. There also has been the usual generous support of the Friends of the Thomas Fisher Rare Book Library.

The range and scope of this exhibition are international in geographical coverage, with a breadth of subject coverage which illustrates the historical emphases of each institution, especially the federated colleges. The beautiful Chinese calligraphy of Wen Zhengming (East Asian) can be compared and contrasted to Harunobu's equally beautiful courtesans of Edo (ROM). Fifteenth-century Europe is represented by Günther Zainer's 1473 edition of Aegidius Romanus, with its distinguished provenance (Trinity) and the important, and rare, 1476 edition of Filelfo's satires (Fisher). The great 1516 Erasmus edition of the New Testament (CRRS) seems a direct influence on Luther's 1520 *Freedom of a Christian*, significantly published in German (Trinity). Cardinal Bellarmine's commentary on the Psalms (Regis) demonstrates that, although he had great political power, he was also a scholar. The oldest item on display is a tenth-century leaf from a book of homilies (Pontifical Institute), something of a contrast to a 1784 letter of John Wesley (United Church Archives). Canada is, of course, well represented, beginning with James Evans' *Cree Syllabic Hymn Book* and a sample of the 1840 type from which it was printed (Victoria). Very different, but no less important, is the 1965 manuscript page of theologian Bernard Lonergan (Lonergan Research Institute). It provides a kind of companion for Henri Nouwen's manuscript of 'L'Arche and the World' (St. Michael's). The faculty of Music provides a whole section of the exhibition with a wonderful range from Luis Milan's 1535 collection of Spanish lute music, through Handel and Gluck, to the *Colonial Harmonist* of 1836.

Theology has been a dominant theme in this exhibition, but the arts and sciences are also represented. Bishop Strachan's copy of Joseph Priestley's work on the discovery of oxygen takes us back to the beginnings of the University in 1827 (Trinity), while Ackermann's *University of Oxford* provides a nineteenth-century glimpse of a much older institution (Fisher-OISE). Not all the exhibits are book and manuscripts and from Victoria, appropriately, come Baxter prints of Queen Victoria's coronation, and the Great Exhibition of 1851. That exhibition also provided the stimulus for Vizetelly & Company's amazing *Statistical Chart* (Massey). The 'Coronation Bible' of 1953 is one of twenty-five copies, the binding designed by Lynton Lamb, presented to Vincent Massey (Fisher-Hart House). Lamb was also a wood engraver, an art and craft represented by the proofs of Agnes Miller Parker's 'The Frogs and Jupiter' from Gregynog Press *Fables of Aesop* (Massey). The original watercolours by Charles Cordiner of eighteenth-century Scottish scenery were turned into engravings for his books (Trinity). Photography is represented in a spectacular way with an example from Edward Curtis' forty volume *The North American Indian*, published between 1907 and 1930 (ROM). Equally amazing, and possibly unique, are the original stereotype moulds of *The Cologne Post* of May 8, 1919, which contain the terms of the Treaty of Versailles, probably the most important political document of the twentieth century (Massey). Art and literature are combined in the works of William Blake from Victoria, which is also renowned for its Coleridge collection and its Bloomsbury holdings, represented here by the first edition of Virginia Woolf's *Mrs. Dalloway*, together with the original art work for the dust jacket by Vanessa Bell.

The discovery and contemplation of the books, manuscripts, and art works for this exhibition has been an exciting experience. The exhibits suggest something of the further rich research resources in this university and it is a privilege for the Fisher Library to provide a window through the walls.

Richard Landon, Director

Contributors to the Catalogue

JB	Jonathan Bengtson
RCB	Robert C. Brandeis
PJC	Pearce Carefoote
LC	Linda Corman
RD	Robert Doran, S.J.
GE	Gabrielle Earnshaw
JF	James Farge, C.S.B.
AG	Alison Girling
JH	Jack Howard
HK	Hana Kim
MK	Marie Korey
RL	Richard Landon
NM	Noel McFerran
KM	Kathleen McMorrow
YP	Yannick Portebois
SQ	Stephen Qiao
SR	Sunhee Ro
DS	Dean Seeman
LS	Lisa Sherlock
AS	Arthur Smith
CKS	Carmen Königsreuther Socknat
DES	Dorothy E. Speirs
KY	Kimberley Yates
LY	Lorna Young
GZ	Gabbi Zaldin

Centre for Reformation and Renaissance Studies, Victoria University in the University of Toronto

In 1886 a young Canadian scholar named Andrew James Bell who was studying in Leipzig purchased a collection of eighty early printed books, mostly by the Dutch humanist Desiderius Erasmus, which had belonged to the German classical philologist Jacob Bernays (1824–1881). Bell was primarily a classicist, and his interest in Erasmus derived from the impact Erasmus had had on the use of the Latin language. In the years after this purchase, Bell's personal library blossomed to over thirty thousand titles, filling every wall and overflowing into the floors and staircases of his ten-room home at 17 Avenue Road, where the Four Seasons Hotel now sits. He tracked his collection in a swollen scrapbook jammed with tiny slips of paper, each of which documented a title, an author, a date, and sometimes a publisher and an indication of where the book was shelved. Bell's death in 1932 brought the entire collection to Victoria College, which lacked the resources to manage such a large bequest. His catalogue was examined in 1933 by George H. Locke, the Chief Librarian of the Public Library of Toronto, who discovered that the collection contained many Erasmus items so rare that they could not even be located in the British Museum. Two hundred and fifty volumes were separated and catalogued by Marie Tremaine. They were displayed for a few years, but eventually, along with the remainder of Bell's early editions of the classics, were stored in less than ideal conditions for almost thirty years. In the early 1960s, F. David Hoeniger, an English professor at Victoria College, recommended that the collection be better managed, and in 1963, a research facility named the Centre for Reformation and Renaissance Studies was formed around the nucleus provided by Bell's collection of Erasmiana and early printed classical texts. Their availability inspired the University of Toronto Press to embark upon a massive publication project in 1969 to translate all of Erasmus's correspondence and principal writings into English. At a projected eighty-six volumes, *The Collected Works of Erasmus* is the largest academic publishing project in Canadian history. The CRRS is now housed in the E.J. Pratt Library. The non-circulating collection holds approximately four thousand rare books and twenty thousand volumes of reference and scholarship on the Renaissance. *KY*

Cheng Yu Tung East Asian Library

Most of the Chinese rare books in the Cheng Yu Tung East Asian Library belong to the Mu Collection, a private collection of scholarly books from Mr. Mu Xuexun (1880–1929). Mu was born in Penglai County, Shandong Province. He graduated from Peiyang University in Tianjin and worked as the Chinese Secretary at the German Legation in Beijing for seventeen years. He spent over twenty-five years building up his personal library, which consisted of roughly forty thousand books. Among them are four volumes of Song (960 - 1279) printed editions, ninety-eight volumes of Yuan (1271–1368) editions, seven volumes of Ming

(1368–1644) manuscripts, 3,413 volumes of Ming editions and 329 volumes of Qing (1644–1911) manuscripts. Some of these are unique and most are rare.

When Mu died in 1929, his son was assigned a position outside of Beijing and so the family decided to sell the collection. Canadian missionary, Bishop William Charles White (1873–1960), offered $10,500 to purchase it in its entirety and his offer was accepted immediately by the Mu family. Additional donations from Dr. Sigmund Samuel, Sir Robert Mond, and Professor John C. Ferguson (all from Toronto) helped White with the purchase. As a result, they proposed to call the collection 'the University of Toronto Chinese Library'. White (whose personal papers are now in the Thomas Fisher Rare Book Library) was the first Anglican Bishop in Henan Province (1901–1930) and the first Canadian bishop to be consecrated for service in the mission field.

Ten Chinese workers were hired to prepare a descriptive catalogue for the library collection. Eighteen volumes were completed in early 1935 (with another twenty-two volumes prepared later in Toronto) after which the collection was ready to sail to Canada. The shipment arrived at the Royal Ontario Museum in June of 1935. At the time, it was the third largest university collection of Chinese books in North America, after the Gest Library at McGill and the Harvard-Yenching Library.

In 1968, the majority of the Mu collection became part of the University of Toronto Libraries' holdings. The East Asiatic Studies Library was created with sixty thousand volumes, half of which belonged to the original Mu collection with the remainder composed of those books added in the years since 1935. The only materials excluded were those relating to art and archaeology.

In 1974, the East Asiatic Studies Library moved to the Robarts building where it was absorbed into the Central Library and renamed simply the 'East Asian Library'. The Mu collection was relocated to its own rare book reading room. In the following years, the East Asian Library participated in the RLG North American Rare Book Cataloguing Project, and a large part of the Mu collection was described and catalogued in detail. The remaining un-catalogued rare books were also listed and information on these is accessible online on the Cheng Yu Tung East Asian Library Home Page. *SQ*

The East Asian Library established the Korean studies collection in 1979 with a grant from the Korean Traders Scholarship Foundation in Toronto. Professor Cha-shin Yu of the Department of East Asian Studies then negotiated a deal for the Library to purchase a collection of Korean duplicate books from the Harvard-Yenching Library. Most of the Korean rare books currently held in the East Asian Library were part of this original acquisition. This rare book collection has eighty titles (214 volumes) in total. Although most of these materials are duplicates from the Harvard-Yenching Library, they are still considered rare worldwide. *HK*

Bernard Lonergan Archives, Lonergan Research Institute

What has become The Bernard Lonergan Archives actually began to be assembled in 1953, when Lonergan was still alive and very active, for it was then that he began to give to Frederick Crowe a number of his papers. Crowe kept these papers until 1970, when he began a Lonergan Centre at Regis College. For fifteen years the Centre consisted of one room in the College, which relocated from Willowdale to downtown Toronto in 1976. That one room housed a library of primary and secondary sources and the papers that Lonergan had given him. More papers were handed over in the early 1970s. In 1985, the Centre expanded into the Lonergan Research Institute, and the library and archives were divided into two rooms. The final installment of papers had come into the care of Crowe and Robert Doran, Trustees of the Lonergan Estate, at the time of Lonergan's death in November of 1984. The Lonergan Archives are located in the Lonergan Research Institute, 10 St. Mary Street, Suite 500, Toronto. The Archives now contain many of Lonergan's papers, plus audio tapes of his lectures, and the books that were in his possession at the time of his death. The papers have been catalogued and filed in accordance with archival practice, and the tapes are being converted to digital format for the sake of preservation.   *RD*

Robertson Davies Library, Massey College

Massey College was built by the Massey Foundation and opened its doors to graduate students of the University of Toronto in 1963. The first Master of the College, Robertson Davies, believed that a library brought distinction to the College and encouraged the development of research collections in the history of printing. With Davies' support, Douglas Lochhead, the first College Librarian, gathered together printing presses and related equipment to establish a bibliographical press. The Massey College Press, as the printing shop is known, has five iron hand presses which are used for teaching purposes to provide students with an understanding of printing technology and book production. The collections of books include material on the history of the book, calligraphy, type design and type specimens, printing (including printers' manuals), papermaking, bookbinding, book collecting, and bibliography. These materials are complemented by the papers of Canadian graphic designers, Carl Dair (1912–1967) and Allan Fleming (1929–1977). In 1969 Lochhead began negotiations to purchase the collection of 'Victorian Book Design and Colour Printing' assembled by Ruari McLean. It was acquired and, with the additions made to it, has become one of the premier collections of its kind in North America, drawing researchers from around the world. In 1981, the Massey College Library was named for the Founding Master upon the occasion of his retirement. Over the years he presented the Library with editions and translations of his writings. The Robertson Davies Library also provides administrative support for the graduate Collaborative Program in Book History and Print Culture which has been based at Massey College since its inception in 1999.   *MK*

Faculty of Music Library

In May 2004, the reading room for Rare Books and Special Collections in the Faculty of Music Library was named the Olnick Room, in honour of the musicologist Harvey Olnick (1917-2003) and his work in shaping and developing the collections in the vault behind it, collections which had their origins in donations to the University of the personal libraries of many nineteenth- and early twentieth-century Toronto musicians.

In the planning for the construction of the Edward Johnson building, the home of the music faculty since 1962, Olnick established a modest rare book room as part of the new library floor, and made the selection of early and significant editions to be housed in it. Working with dealers in New York, and supported by the Associates of the University of Toronto there, he decided to pursue substantive holdings in seventeenth- and eighteenth-century French opera scores, in order to complement the Fisher Library's libretto collections. He also acquired representative examples of Canadian sheet music, and of early English vocal and instrumental publications, and made donations from his own library of Italian baroque music.

Library staff have continued to build the collections on these foundations, so that undergraduates may study examples of the variety of formats of western art music, from medieval liturgical manuscripts, through first editions of Mozart quartets, to the outsized limited edition score of Poul Ruder's opera *The Handmaid's Tale* (based on the novel by Margaret Atwood), while a performer may locate a rare source for the theatre music of Purcell, and a scholar do historical research in the archives of Kathleen Parlow.

The importance of donations remains undiminished. For example, in 1973, among Sidney Fisher's gifts to the University were early flute publications and music histories. In the 1980s, several grants from the SSHRC program for Specialized Research Collections further strengthened the French opera and Canadian music holdings. Since the 1990s, composers and jazz musicians associated with the faculty have deposited their papers in the expanded space in the Edwards Wing.   *KM*

Pontifical Institute of Mediaeval Studies

Opened in 1929, the Institute library now holds about 110,000 books on medieval culture and subscribes to two hundred specialized journals – all shelved in non-circulating open stacks. Its Special Collections have been acquired to support the research of its Fellows and its MSL teaching program, which require interdisciplinary familiarity with medieval philosophy, theology, history, law, liturgy, literature, art, and archaeology – as well as skill in palaeography. Early printed books and many multi-volume folio sets were purchased when market prices were still low, while later acquisitions of rare materials have come from gifts and bequests. In lieu of buying expensive original manuscripts, the Fellows ordered the microfilming of nearly nine thousand manuscripts from over five hundred different libraries and archives. A recent special donation has allowed the purchase of eight hundred CD-ROMs and DVDs containing the images of all the papal letters written between 1198 and 1464. In recent years, the library has received gifts of large libraries focusing on Byzantine theology, Spanish liturgy and art, English monasticism, and nature in the Middle Ages, as well as many facsimiles of illuminated manuscripts from the Vatican Library.   *JF*

Regis College Library

Regis originated as the Jesuit Seminary/College of Christ the King in downtown Toronto in 1930, offering a program of undergraduate studies in philosophy, arts, and sciences for English-speaking Canadian Jesuits. A program in theology was added in 1943. In 1961, the College relocated to a new facility in North York. The identity of Regis changed dramatically in 1969 when it became a founding member of the new Toronto School of Theology, an ecumenical federation of seven theological faculties and colleges offering graduate degrees in theology. In 1976 Regis College relocated to 15 St. Mary St. to be in closer proximity to the other theological colleges and the University of Toronto.

Regis College Library began as the Jesuit Seminary library, following the mandate of St. Ignatius Loyola (1491–1556), founder of the Society of Jesus, that there should be a library in each Jesuit college. Prior to the relocation to St. Mary St. and the admission of the first lay student to the College in 1976, the faculty and student body of the College had been entirely Jesuit and the Library's collections and operations had been designed for a residential Jesuit community. Subsequent to the relocation, the Library was opened to the University of Toronto community and its holdings were added to the union catalogue of the University of Toronto Libraries. Regis College Library has a solid theological collection of approximately a hundred thousand volumes and is an excellent resource for classic Christian texts in their original languages and in translation. The collection is also strong in Christian spirituality (with a specialization in the Spiritual Exercises of St. Ignatius), Christian ethics, and Roman Catholic systematic and historical theology.   *LY*

Royal Ontario Museum Library Rare Book Collections

On 5 October 1981 the ROM Library re-opened to the public in its new home in the newly-constructed Curatorial Centre. Within the new Library, space was dedicated to the rare book collections for the first time. Fondly referred to as 'The Cage', the secured area housed many of the rare titles acquired over the previous sixty-seven-year history of the ROM. Until then the rare books were retained in the departmental offices, workrooms, and collection rooms of the Museum. Today the rare book collections include over four thousand titles devoted to the decorative arts, architecture and design, discovery and exploration, natural history, ethnology, textiles, and fashion. The R.S. Williams collection of rare music scores was one of the first acquisitions, dating from 1913. While small donations trickled in during the early years of the Museum, it was the J.H. Fleming collection of ornithology and natural history books that substantially augmented the rare book collections in the 1930s. Another major donation, which came to the Museum, in 1974, was the Robert Baldwin Fordyre Barr collection of books on architecture and design, which greatly enriched the rare book collections' holdings in support of curatorial research in the decorative arts. The Sigmund Samuel collection of rare Canadiana titles was maintained as a separate collection housed in the Canadiana building, on the University of Toronto campus, until the late 1990s, when it was relocated to the Museum's main building on Queen's Park Crescent. It continues to be housed with the Canadiana collection of prints and drawings, and includes such notable titles as J.F.W. Des Barres' 'Atlantic Neptune' and Theodore de Bry's works on exploration from the 1590s. The rare book collections at the ROM are added to on an annual basis principally through donation. One of the most recent acquisitions was James Sowerby's thirty-six volume 'English Botany' (1790–1814), profusely illustrated with hand-coloured botanical engravings, donated by Dr. Noel Hynes in 2005. *AS*

The Far Eastern Library of the Royal Ontario Museum, named the H.H. Mu Far Eastern Library, in honour of the founding collection, has a rare book collection of around seven hundred items. It was probably around 1930 that Bishop William Charles White, first Keeper of the ROM's Chinese collections, learned of a significant collection of the Chinese classics of art, science, and literature that had become available in Beijing. Mu Xuexun, Secretary to the German Legation, had spent years assembling this collection, which included Ming dynasty manuscripts. Mr. Mu had died in 1929; his family stipulated the collection remain intact in an institution of higher learning as a memorial to their father. Bishop White met those conditions; they closed the sale in 1933. The collection was catalogued in Beijing over the next few years and then shipped to the ROM. The 'H.H. Mu Chinese Library' opened in 1937. The Mu Library now forms the basis of the present collections of rare books in both the ROM's Far Eastern Library and the University of Toronto's Cheng Yu Tung East Asian Library. The Far Eastern Library collection has grown over the years in size and diversity. It now includes books in Chinese, Japanese, Korean, and Western Languages. It has been added to primarily through gifts, but a number of rare books germane to the ROM's artefact collections have been acquired through purchase. *JH*

John M. Kelly Library, St. Michael's College

The core collection of the University of St. Michael's College dates to the founding of the College in the mid-nineteenth century. The Soulerin Collection, a collection of some seven hundred monographs, honours Rev. Jean Mathieu Soulerin, founding Superior of St. Michael's College, 1852–1865. The development of special collections at St Michael's is closely related to the construction of the John M. Kelly Library at the University of St. Michael's College in 1969. The Counter-Reformation Collection was established that same year and assembles the works of Catholic thinkers who were of central importance in the history of the Church from the Council of Trent to the French Revolution. It is generally recognized as one of the strongest Counter-Reformation collections in North America.

In 1976 the John M. Kelly Library took the first steps towards the development of what would eventually become the Joseph Sablé Centre for 19th Century French Studies. In that year, Rev. J. Sablé, Associate Professor of French at the University of Toronto and lifelong book collector, offered to donate his extensive collection of books on the Romantic Movement in France to St. Michael's College. In 1995 when the collection was relocated to a new research centre within the library, room was also provided for the Zola Collection, which had been created in support of the publication of the correspondence of Emile Zola. The work on this collection is ongoing and the Centre is now also the locus of the Book & Media Studies program at St. Michael's College. In 2001, the Centre won the Northrop Frye Award.

The John Henry Cardinal Newman Collection at the Kelly Library is the largest collection of early editions of Newman's works in North America. It reflects the writing and influence of John Henry Cardinal Newman, the English theologian and writer who led the Anglican Oxford Movement before converting to Catholicism in 1845. The collection began as a donation in 1973 from Reverend Cyril W. Sullivan, a priest from Brampton, Ontario, and now includes the collections of Hugh Fraser McIntosh, the Reverend Peter Sheehan, Monsignor Richard O'Brien, and the Reverend James C. Carberry. In late 2005, another extensive and important donation was received from the estate of Douglas Ellory Pett, an Anglican priest and Newman scholar from Cornwall, England. The Kelly Library is currently coordinating an international effort to digitize the complete corpus of early works by and about Newman. In the same year that the Newman Collection was established, the Library also received its first of many donations of material related to G.K. Chesterton. The Chesterton collection is now regarded as the finest in Canada. More recently, in the year 2000, St. Michael's accepted the archive of Henri Nouwen, considered one of the greatest spiritual writers of the late twentieth century. This collection was soon augmented by material from L'Arche Daybreak and the Faith & Sharing organization. In May 2006, the Library hosted the first ever international conference assessing Nouwen's life and legacy.

The Kelly Library now has a diverse range of special collections that attracts researchers from around the world and are used increasingly as pedagogical resources for the College's own undergraduate programs in Book & Media Studies, Celtic Studies, Medieval Studies, and Christianity & Culture. In 2006 the Kelly Library will begin processing its latest major acquisitions – substantial materials related to Marshall McLuhan (who taught for many years at St. Michael's) and the manuscripts and papers of the Canadian writer Sheila Watson.   JB

John W. Graham Library, Trinity College

The origin of special collections in Trinity College's John W. Graham Library pre-dates the College itself. In 1828 John Strachan secured a collection of theological books from the Church of England's Society for the Promotion of Christian Knowledge to stock the library of his projected University of King's College in Upper Canada, an entity that ultimately became the secular University of Toronto. When Trinity College opened its doors in 1852 this collection was returned to the 'Church University' where it has remained the founding collection supporting Anglican studies at Trinity. At the same time, Bishop Strachan himself donated a large number of books to the library on a wide range of subjects, which, together with the later bequest of his personal library, became known as the Strachan Collection. Over the years other rare books have been added, chiefly in the areas of Anglican church history, liturgy, and theology, including most recently a comprehensive collection of the works of Richard Hooker, acquired through the generosity of David and Mary Neelands and W. Speed Hill, the scholar-editor who initially formed the collection. Special collections also include the published works of noted Trinity authors, such as Archibald Lampman, Henry Youle Hind, Sir Gilbert Parker, Dorothy Livesay, and Austin Clarke. An important collection of the writings of Sir Winston Churchill was donated by the Churchill Society for the Advancement of Parliamentary Democracy in the 1980s and has been subsequently enhanced by major donations from Anne and Frederick Stinson and F. Bartlett and Lucienne Watt. This collection includes rare printed items, holograph letters, memorabilia, and the extensive source material used by David Dilks for his recent study of Churchill's visits to Canada. A unique collection of materials emanating from the G7/G8 Economic Summits and collected on site since 1988 by Professor John Kirton's G8 Research Group reflects the Graham Library's current commitment to supporting the International Relations Program and the University of Toronto web-based G8 Information Centre. Thanks to the gifts of Guy and Sandra Upjohn the Graham Library is acquiring the extraordinary collection of important printed works from the fifteenth to the twentieth centuries originally assembled by distinguished Toronto bookman J. Kemp Waldie.

LC

United Church Archives/Victoria University Archives

The United Church of Canada Archives, Canada's largest religious archive, document the history of the United Church of Canada and its antecedent denominations. The United Church of Canada was established in 1925 with the union of the Methodist, Presbyterian, and Congregational Churches, later joined by the eastern Canadian Conference of the Evangelical United Brethren in 1968. The United Church Archives established their base at Victoria University (an institution tied in its origins to the Methodist

Church in Canada) in 1953. The Archives occupied several buildings before moving to its present quarters, renovated for this purpose, in the Birge-Carnegie Library in 1972. In 1985 the Archives assumed responsibility for the Victoria University records, creating the United Church of Canada/Victoria University Archives. The collection consists of documents, correspondence, reports, minutes, church registers, graphic, audio-visual, and printed materials, clippings, and publications of the United Church of Canada and its antecedent denominations; records of the Boards, Departments, and courts of the above denominations; and the records of Victoria University and its constituent colleges, Victoria College and Emmanuel College. University records include those of the governing bodies, administrative offices, student organizations, alumni associations, and other campus organizations. The collection also includes various records of the global mission personnel of the United Church and its antecedents; records of ecumenical and inter-church bodies relating to subjects such as temperance and prohibition, religion in schools, religious education, and social action; and papers of individuals and organizations affiliated with the United Church or Victoria University. *SR*

Victoria University Library

With more than sixty named special collections of books, prints, manuscripts, and archives in the broad subject areas of art, Canadiana, literature, politics, and religious studies, Victoria University Library provides significant research materials to the University of Toronto and to the international scholarly community. Special Collections at Victoria can be said to have begun in the late 1850s and 1860s when Methodist missionaries, lay preachers, and others connected to the College donated ethnographic material collected on their travels. These collections were enhanced by artefacts collected by Charles Trick Currelly (1876–1957), later director of the Royal Ontario Museum, and by the diaries, field notebooks, journals, sketches, and paintings created by his favourite professor, A.P. Coleman (1852–1939), the first director of the Royal Ontario Museum of Geology. Coleman's sister, Helen (1860–1953), a musician and writer, bequeathed her archive to join that of her brother and thus established family archives as a feature of Special Collections at Victoria. The E.J. Pratt manuscripts along with the papers of his wife Viola Whitney Pratt, and the manuscripts and prints of their daughter Claire Pratt, are the basis of much scholarly research and publication, including a web-based hypertext approach to an edition of E.J. Pratt's poetry.

The collection of George Baxter nineteenth-century prints and illustrated books, given by Anne C.M. Starr in memory of her husband Fredrick Newton Gisborne Starr, was later joined by the Gisborne papers and diaries relating to the development of the first transatlantic cable. Mary Rowell Jackman began and endowed continuing support for the Library's Virginia Woolf/ Hogarth Press/ Bloomsbury Collection. Numbering more than three thousand items and encompassing all aspects of the Bloomsbury Group's creative and decorative arts, the collection is considered to be the best of its kind in the world.

The story of the internationally significant Samuel Taylor Coleridge Collection brought to Victoria by Prof. Kathleen Coburn is a fascinating adventure related in her autobiographical work *In Pursuit of Coleridge* (1977). This collection became the genesis of the thirty-three-volume *Collected Works of Samuel Taylor Coleridge*, a thirty-year editorial project headquartered in the Library at Victoria. Major scholarly editorial work also centres on the Northrop Frye Archive and collection of more than 2,500 annotated books from his personal library. Frye's archive and especially his work on the artist, poet, and visionary William Blake form a useful complement to the important, recently acquired, Bentley Collection of William Blake and his Contemporaries.

Many of the rare and important books in the Andrew James Bell Collection of more than thirty thousand volumes were added to the Library, and his collection of books by Erasmus became the nucleus of the Centre for Reformation and Renaissance Studies located in the E.J. Pratt Library. In 1921 Sir John Eaton presented Victoria with the John and Charles Wesley Collection formed by bibliographer Richard Green; with additions over the years this is now one of the two most comprehensive Wesley collections in North America.

Primary source materials within other collections at the Library encompass such subjects as philosophy, the circus, and modern poets and dramatists. The research utility of Victoria's Special Collections and the possibilities for scholarship continue to grow at Victoria with, for example, the recent acquisition of the archive of film director and producer Norman Jewison.   *RCB*

EAST ASIAN COLLECTIONS

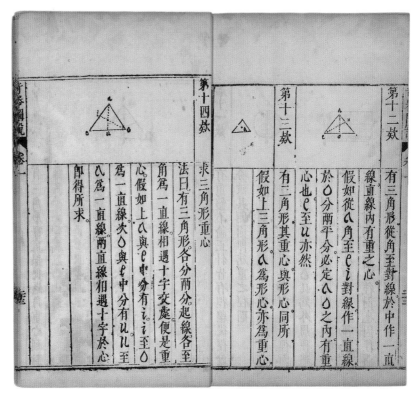

右側頁：

第十二欵

有三角形從角至對線於中作一直
線直線內有重心
假如從A角至Ci對線作一直線
於C分兩平分必定AO之內有重
心也C至u亦然
有三角形其重心與形心同所
假如上三角形A爲形心亦爲重心

第十三欵

左側頁：

第十四欵　求三角形重心
法曰有三角形各分兩分起線各至
角爲一直線相遇十字交處便是重
心假如上三角A與C中分有i至O
爲一直線次AO與C中分有ul至
A爲一直線兩直線相遇十字於心
即得所求

上部（草書）：

寧音楚⋯更家越軟圍核
仿途滅補跡土會盟何
遵約法歸故頃刑起富
頃牧用軍甲鵜宮城沙
洋馳譽丹青九州秀蹟
百形泰箏莊宗泰岱禪
主云亭爲門崇室涂田
赤城昌池碣石禋壁洞

文徵 明:《文徵明行書千字文》, 1534?

Wen Zhengming

Wen Zhengming xing shu qian zi wen. 1534?

This is a Chinese calligraphy work in cursive script by one of the four great masters of the art in the Ming Dynasty, Wen Zhengming (1470–1559). Wen was born in Suzhou, Jiangsu Province, where the important 'Wu art school' emerged during the Ming Dynasty. Wen himself learned his calligraphy from Huang Gongwang (1269–1354), a Yuan master of calligraphy who specialized in regular and cursive scripts as well as other styles. The talents of Wen Zhengming were well-represented in a number of the arts, and he particularly excelled at painting, calligraphy, poetry, and essay writing. His *Qian zi wen* (*Thousand Character Text,*) in four typical calligraphic styles (seal, clerical, cursive, and standard) is considered one of the best works in Chinese calligraphic history; the *Wen Zhengming xing shu qian zi wen* is one example of the cursive style. The book has a 'butterfly' binding, meaning that it is a double-leaved album with black paper rubbing plates mounted onto each leaf. The rubbings replicate the original calligraphic text in a superior manner and the ink shines black against the irregular light-grey patterned background. Most of the character strokes have sharp edges indicating that the rubbings were made shortly after the carving of the stele. The stele was definitely engraved later than the date of the calligraphy, making this the primary text.

SQ

王徵:《新制諸器圖說》, 萬頃堂, 1627 (1816 年版)

Joannes Terentius, Wang Zheng

Yuan xi qi qi tu shuo lu zui and *Xin zhi zhu qi tu shuo*. Published by Wang qian tan, 1627 (1816 printing).

This was the first book printed in China to introduce Western mechanical inventions and engineering to the country, an event that occurred during the Ming Dynasty (1368–1644). The book is in two parts; Part one is a translation of an oral account by the German missionary Joannes Terentius, with illustrations by Wang Zheng. It presents key Western concepts of mathematics, physics, and technology as understood in seventeenth-century Europe. Joannes Terentius (1575–1630), also known as Johannes Schreck, and by his Chinese name Deng Yuhan, was a lawyer's son, born in Konstanz, Southern Germany. A Jesuit, he studied at the University of Padua in Northern Italy and was stationed in China about the year 1618. In addition he was a gifted astronomer and physicist, elected as the seventh member of the Cesi Academy, just after Galileo. Wang Zheng (1571–1644), on the other hand, held the degree of 'jinshi', the quasi-doctoral degree in the Chinese imperial examination system of the late Ming Dynasty. He passed the official examinations only at the age of fifty-two. Under the influence of his father, who was a teacher of mathematics and medicine, Wang became fascinated with Western science and technology after coming into contact with missionaries in Beijing, where he had traveled many times for his examinations. In order for Wang Zhen to make technical European texts available to his countrymen, he needed Terentius' help. The result of this collaboration in 1627 was the *Yuan xi qi qi tu shuo lu zui* (*Collected Diagrams and Explanations of Wonderful Machines from the Far West*) of 1627, which was a compilation of several European texts that Wang Zhen thought were most practical for the Chinese people. The book was the first in China to explain the basics of mechanics and practical machinery. The pages measure twenty-six centimetres in height, and contain nine vertical lines with eighteen characters per line including punctuation. Fine illustrations detail the geometric principles associated with the various machines under discussion. The current edition was printed in the twenty-first year of the Jiaqing reign (1816), and is based on an earlier 1627 version from the seventh year of the Tianqi reign, Ming Dynasty.　　　　　　　　　　　　　　　　　　　　　　　　　　　*SQ*

3

Cheng Yu Tung
East Asian Library

于朋舉:《玉堂才調集》, 清芬堂, 1699
Yu Pengju
Yu tang cai diao ji. Qing fen tang, 1699.

This book, from the original Mu collection, was compiled by Yu Pengju, and contains over three thousand poems written in the period between the Tang Dynasty (618–907) and the Ming Dynasty (1368–1644). The editor learned Chinese classical poetry from the early Qing scholars, Wu Meicun and Song Chaixue, and collected regulated verse poems from the Tang Dynasty and its successors. After travelling to several provinces over the years, Yu expanded his collection to several thousand poems. He believed poetry provided one of the most effective ways of educating ordinary people about high moral standards. The book came out in limited editions and modern reprints, with the editor arranging the poetry according to rhythmic entries (a total of thirty sections) set by *Pei wen yun fu* (*Phrases, Rhymes, and Phonology in Collection*). A seal stamped on the cover page of volume one, 'Wan juan lou cong shu', indicates that the book formed part of one of the most famous private libraries in Jiangsu Province. Two other printed stamps after the preface read 'Yu Pengju yin' and 'Nian an'. There is another collection of poems published under the same title by Wei Hu of the Sixth Dynasty (tenth century).　　　　　　　　　　　　　　　　　　　　　　　*SQ*

4

Cheng Yu Tung
East Asian Library

七十一 (椿園):《西域聞見錄 》, 1777
Qishiyi (Chunyuan)
Xi yu wen jian lu. 1777.

This is one of the best travel records of the Xi yu (or Xiyu), the western frontier during the Qing Dynasty that includes the contemporary Xinjiang Uygur Autonomous Region and parts of Gansu as well as the Qinghai Province. The author Chunyuan (Qishiyi), a Manchurian traveller, lived in Xinjiang for many years and explored the region thoroughly. The detailed descriptions of the territory's geographical characteris-

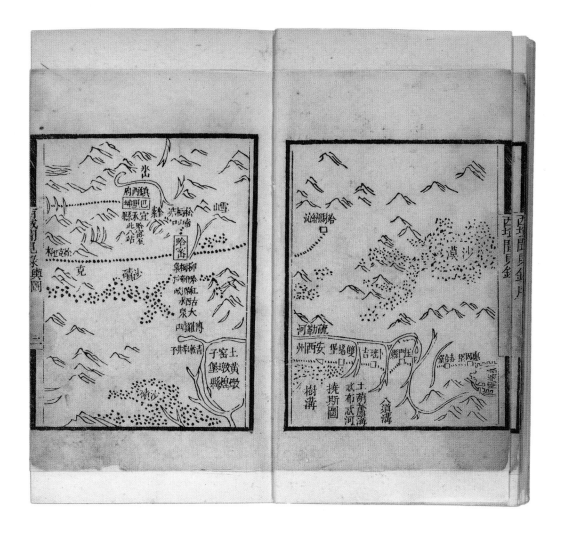

tics, natural resources, historical background, and minority peoples and their customs, present the readers with an intimate account of Xi yu. The book has eight chapters that provide a general introduction to the different areas of Xinjiang together with a detailed description of its inhabitants, including ethnic minorites, and major historical events with special reference to those events concerning the Qing emperor Qianlong's suppression of the rebellion of the local tribes. Four leaves of hand-drawn maps supply details of geographical data about Xi yu for the first time. Because of its value and significance, the text has been reprinted many times. The library's copy is a rare early edition. According to the author's preface, the book was published in the forty-second year of Qianlong's reign (1777). It was remounted in China for preservation purposes with new and slightly longer leaves of rice paper inserted between the originals. The printers adopted a layout of eight vertical lines of type with sixteen characters per line. A pair of seals appears in the middle of volume one and again in volume four as proof of ownership. This and later editions of the title are held by the China National Library. The Cheng Yu Tung East Asian Library holds other copies of this item under different titles (Xi yu ji, 1814; Xi yu zong zhi, 1966). The book was also translated into Russian in 1823 and 1829, and into French in 1887. *SQ*

陳倫炯:《海國聞見錄》, 1793?

Chen Lunjiong

Hai guo wen jian lu. 1793?

This title, which formed part of the original Mu library, is recognized as one of the best published works about the lands and peoples of Korea, Japan, Taiwan, and the islands in Southeast Asia by a Chinese author during the Qing Dynasty (1644–1911). The six maps in the book demonstrate the advanced skills of Chinese navigators in making admiralty and hydrographic charts in the 1700s. The author, Chen Lunjiong (1703–1730), was a Qing general posted in Taiwan and Zhejiang Province during the reigns of Emperor Yongzheng and Qianlong (1723–1795). Under the influence of his father Chen Ang, who was a sea trader in Southeast Asia for many years, Chen developed an early interest in the sea, and the islands of coastal China and Southeast Asia. The eight chapters of this book are divided into general descriptions of coastal China, the 'East Sea' (Korea, Japan), the 'Southeast Sea', the 'South Sea', the 'Minor West Sea', the 'Major West Sea', 'Kunlun', and 'Nan Ao qi' along with maps. The current revised edition, published in the fifty-eighth year of Emperor Qianlong in Zhejiang province in 1793, has two new prefaces that emphasize the importance of China's coastal defence. They also provide information about the peoples and cultures that existed at the time beyond China's borders. Seven maps depict the Qing Empire's position in the world and the locations of the East and Southeast Asian countries as they were known at the time. India, central Asia, Europe and Africa also appear in the maps. The complete coast line of China and the offshore islands from the northeast to the south were recorded in great detail. The geography of Taiwan was also depicted in a separate map. Only a few academic libraries in North America (Harvard, Stanford) have this edition in their collections.

SQ

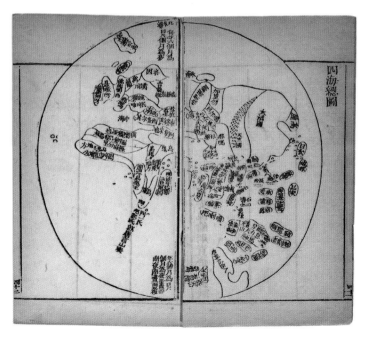

卷一   子時東北寅位。

六

6　　《六壬圖像》，　清代.

Cheng Yu Tung　　*Liu ren tu xi ang*

East Asian Library　　<u>Q</u>ing Dynasty.

This manuscript is a traditional Chinese astrological text containing images of the deities most closely associated with the earth, together with detailed divination instructions applied to various circumstances. The so called *'liu ren'* (the six possible combinations of the Heavenly Stems and Earthly Branches) was evolved from *Yi jing* (*The Book of Changes*) and developed as the main branch of the ancient Chinese 'way of counting' ('shu shu'). The principle of *liu ren* is derived from the twelve earthly branches of the Chinese lunar calendar system that defines the universe as a heavenly disc and an earthly disc. Each disc is equally divided into twelve sections called the twelve palaces (gong), and each palace has its particular orientation and its own representative deity. In this scheme, divination uses the simultaneous occurrence of both the heavenly palace and the earthly palace at a certain time of a given month to predict good or bad luck, and thereby to advise people in their daily activities. In *Liu ren tu xiang*, divination covers such matters as the weather, military campaigns, individual fortune, wish lists, travel, marriage, illness, dreams, and residential feng-shui, etc. According to the official rules developed during the Qing dynasty (1644–1911), only certain types of astrological books were allowed to be published and distributed, *Liu ren* among them. Based on this information and the physical characteristics of the set, it would appear that this manuscript was probably produced during the Qing period. The twenty-four volumes are housed in five protective cases. The characters display a regular script and are written within printed red grids on thick rice paper, with consistent black ink brushes throughout the book. Fine colour illustrations of the earthly deities in different positions with splendid costumes appear at the beginning of each divination section. There is no other recorded holding of this title.

SQ

7

Cheng Yu Tung
East Asian Library

《四聲精辯》, 19 世紀　《四聲辯異》, 19 世紀
Si sheng jing bian and *Si sheng bian yi*
Nineteenth cent.

Si sheng jing bian is a phonological work on the importance of tonal differentiation in Mandarin Chinese. Proper tone distinction is the first and most important step in the composition of traditional Chinese poetry. Without a working knowledge of the differences between the four principal (and elusive) tones, one cannot hope to master the art of writing poetry. Tones and tonal patterns have been recognized as the crucial element in the creation of Chinese poetry since at least the fifth century. Tonal patterns were strictly observed in Tang poetry (618-906). In addition, 'Lü shi' (regulated verse) and 'jue ju' (broken off lines) have become two of the most important conventions of Chinese classical poetry since then. Both styles require strict tonal arrangements of the lines. For these reasons, phonological handbooks and manuals were in high demand among the literati and the social elite. As the preface to 'Si sheng bian yi' states, 'the same character with different pronunciations must mean that a single character conveys different meanings. One must express the different meanings of the same character in different tones or rhymes.' The authorship of the current volume is unknown. Based on the texture of the paper and the colours, the setting of the type, as well as the font style, the printing of the book can be roughly dated to the nineteenth century. The portable format (9.5 X 4 cm.) suits the book's use as a phonological reference manual. Indeed, it is among the smallest books printed in nineteenth-century China. The quality of the printing and binding is superior with double threads used to ensure greater durability. This title appears only in the China National Library rare book collection; no other copy is held by a North American institution. It forms part of Mu's original scholarly library.

SQ

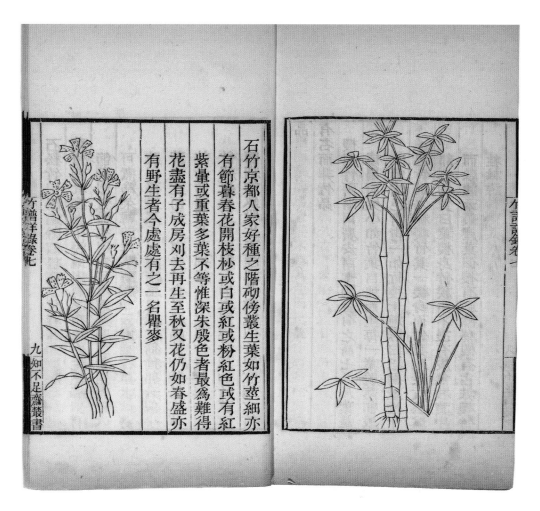

8

李 衍: 《竹譜 詳錄》, 1808

Li Kan: *Zhu pu xiang lu*. 1808.

This handbook of Chinese painting technique, part of the original Mu collection, focuses specifically on the artistic depiction of the bamboo plant. The author, Li Kan (1245–1320), was one of the most famous painters of the early Yuan Dynasty (1271–1368). The most common subject in his paintings is bamboo, and his masterpieces have been collected by the Beijing Palace Museum, the Nanjing Museum, and the Nelson-Atkins Museum of Art in Kansas City. He spent time in Vietnam and South China examining the different species of this plant, and in this book he details both their variety and the techniques used to illustrate them in diverse painting styles. The *Zhu pu xiang lu* is an example of the so-called 'model painting books' (*hua pu*), a major category of books in Chinese art history, which generally concentrate on a single subject such as pine, bamboo, or plum. This book is one of the earliest examples of this type of publication. Printed in the late Qing Dynasty (Jiaqing wuchen 1808) in Anhui Province, this work is based on an earlier Ming Chenghua (1466–1487) edition. It is part of Bao Tingbo's (1728 - 1814) *Zhi bu zu zhai cong shu* (*The Known Deficiencies House series*), which contains over two hundred rare titles printed in the early 1800s. SQ

六角堂池坊
専養

9

新選瓶花図彙　　山中忠左衛門

Shinsen heika zui

(An Illustrated New Selection of Free-Style Flower Arrangements).
Kyoto: Yamanaka Chūzaemon, Genroku 2 [1689].

This book is one of the ten classics of early flower arranging literature. A fine example of quality printing of the early Edo period (1600–1868), it is unique in that the names of the flower arrangements, the post-script, and the outlines of the flowers and vases are printed by woodblock. The beautiful colours of the flowers, leaves, and branches have been added by hand. (Multi-colour printing technology was not developed in Japan until nearly a century later.) Displayed are flower arrangements of the Grand Masters of the Ikenobō School of Flower Arranging from the Azuchi-Momoyama and early Edo periods (ca. 1550–1690). Among the masters represented are Ikenobō Senkō I (1536?–1621), Senzon, Senyō, and the famous pupil of Senyō, Senkō II (1570?–1658). The arrangements are of the *nageire* ('to throw or fling into') style. This austere and simple style was developed for use in the Tea Ceremony. The arrangements illustrated in this book may show elements of a new form of arrangement called *shōka* ('living flower') which was emerging about the time the book was published. *Shōka* combines the dignity of the traditional Buddhist-based *rikka* ('standing flowers') style with the simplicity of *nageire*. *Shōka* was to become the most popular style by the end of the eighteenth century. This book was published in the Genroku era. The period was marked by the burgeoning of *chōnin* (townsmen) culture and a time of general affluence under relaxed government rule. Improved printing techniques had been introduced from Korea. An emphasis on education led to a rise in literacy, which in turn led to a rapid increase in the demand for woodblock printed books. (Movable type printing had been attempted earlier but was generally rejected because it obliterated the aesthetic aspects of the Japanese written language. Movable type remained in limited use for government publications written in Chinese.) Undoubtedly, this book helped to spread interest in flower arranging among the thriving merchant class. It also represents a move away from the strict association of flower arranging with Buddhism. As well, the very existence of this book shows that the economy could now support such elaborate and costly publications.

JH

10

鈴木春信　絵本青楼美人合

Suzuki Harunobu (1725?–1770)

Ehon seirō bijin awase (Illustrated Book of Beauties of the Yoshiwara District). Edo:
Funaki Kasuke [et al.], Meiwa 7 [1770].

Suzuki Harunobu produced this book in the last year of his life. *Seirō* refers to the Yoshiwara licensed district of Edo (now Tokyo). Consequently, the title of the book can also be read *Ehon Yoshiwara Bijin Awase*. It was published in five volumes with portraits of one hundred and sixty-six famous Yoshiwara courtesans. Shown here is the last page of the fifth volume. On the right is one of the *Bijin* or 'Beauties' about to

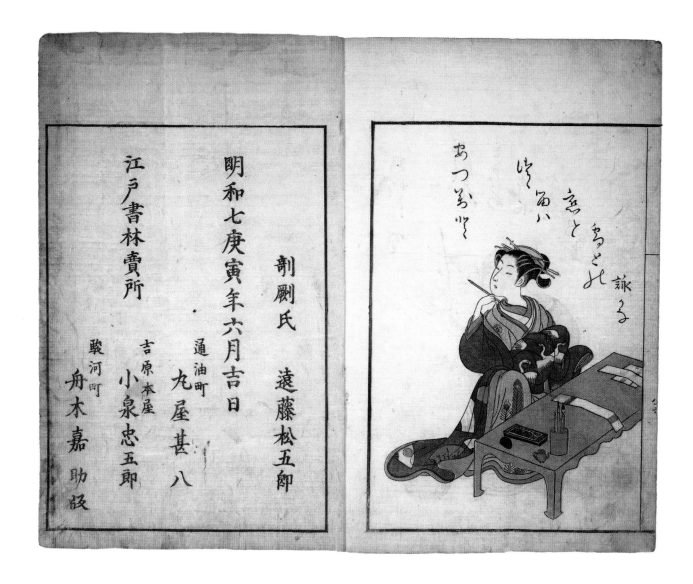

inscribe a poem. The writing above her states that she is pondering whilst looking at the snow, just before putting brush to paper. On the writing table are some *tanzaku* (special heavy paper for writing poems in calligraphy), an inkstone, an ink stick, a water dropper (to wet the stone prior to rubbing the ink stick), and a bamboo stand for holding brushes. The pattern of her kimono tells us that it is the New Year's celebration. Finger and thumb smudging on the lower right provides evidence of substantial handling. On the left is the colophon. From right to left are the name of the engraver, Endō Matsugōrō, the date – seventh year of the Meiwa era – and the names of the Edo booksellers/publishers that produced and carried the book: Maruya Jinpachi, Koizumi Nakagōrō and Funaki Kasuke. The Koizumi Nakagōrō store is in the Yoshiwara district itself. The names of the artist and the main publisher, Funaki Kasuke, are stated on the general title page of the work.

Although at first glance this may appear to be just another colour-illustrated book, it is quite important in the history of *ukiyoe* ('floating world picture') colour-printed books. Harunobu was the originator of *nishikie*, or 'brocade print' multicolour printing using a series of woodblocks for the different colours. He developed this process for the *ukiyoe* prints in 1765. This may have been the first book printed in *nishikie* style. He wished to show that these women were indeed beautiful, not just in their physical beauty, but also in their accomplishments in learning and culture. Ozaki Kyūya, a famous twentieth-century writer on Edo culture, once said that in this book Harunobu was attempting to convey a sense that these women of the Meiwa era were upright like fresh and refined lotus blossoms growing out of the mud. In his last year Harunobu opened up a whole new world of *ukiyoe*. Greatly influential, he remains to this day one of the most popular *ukiyoe* artists.

JH

11

東麓　繪本輪廻物語　畠山照月　畠山保躬

Tōroku

Ehon rinne monogatari (An Illustrated Tale of *Samsāra*). Illustrated by Hatakeyama Shōgetsu. [s.l. : s.n.], Bunsei 2 [1819].

This book, the full title of which is *Abe-no-Nakamaro shōji ruten rinne monogatari* or *Tales of Vicissitudes and Fate in the Life and Death of Abe-no-Nakamaro*, was published in 1819, and concerns the life and afterlife of Abe-no-Nakamaro. It was written by Tōroku and illustrated by Hatakeyama Shōgetsu, who also used the name Hatakeyama Hōkyū. Some scholars believe that Tōroku and Hatakeyama are the same person, Tōroku being the name Hatakeyama used in his medical practice. Both the text and the illustrations are printed from woodblocks. Each woodblock leaf represents two pages of text. In the middle of the block leaf is the title and page number. When the paper is folded, this title and page number fold over from one side of the leaf to the other. The folded leaf is bound at the open edges to form two pages. These are sewn together with simple covers (but with embossed designs) made of heavy layered paper. The five-volume set may have been in a *chitsu* wrapper originally, or perhaps it was first issued in a stiff paper envelope, now lost.

Ehon rinne monogatari is a novel in the *yomihon* genre. *Yomihon* means 'reading books', to distinguish them from the popular illustrated books. Perhaps one could say that *yomihon* are the equivalent of fine illustrated novels of today, as opposed to comic books. In the late eighteenth and early nineteenth centuries, when this genre made its appearance, *yomihon* were considered to be for a sophisticated, literate, and well educated audience. Their appearance also coincided with the rise in the prosperity of the *chōnin* culture (urban culture) and a move away from the predominance of the samurai and court cultures. Although the story is based on an actual historical personage, it has a didactic, moralistic plot incorporating many ghostly and mythical elements. *Yomihon* were modelled after similar Chinese stories of the Ming and Qing dynasties. Each volume or chapter of the *Ehon rinne monogatari* depicts an episode of the tale of Abe-no-Nakamaro. The first volume has a title page, frontispieces illustrating the principal characters in the

stories, and a table of contents for each volume. At the end of the fifth volume is a list of other *yomihon* available from the same publisher.

Abe-no-Nakamaro (698-770) was a Nara-period noble and poet who, in 716, was sent by the Japanese government to study at the Chinese Tang court in Chang'an. He was favoured by the Emperor Xuanzong (685-762) and eventually became a Chinese government official. He spent the final fifty years of his life serving the Tang court, for a time as the governor-general of Vietnam. He attempted to return to Japan once, in 753, but was shipwrecked. In Japan Abe-no-Nakamaro is remembered for his poetry. His name is universally recognized because he is one of the poets of the *Ogura Hyakunin Isshu* (Single Poems by 100 Poets). These poems form a game of one hundred cards that is still played today. His poem expresses melancholy; he knows he will never see his homeland again.   *JH*

12

Cheng Yu Tung
East Asian Library

징보 언 간독

Chingbo ŏn kandok, [s.l. : s.n., 1886?]

This book is an enlarged edition of *Ŏn kandok* (*Korean Letter Writing*) and was widely read in the late Chosŏn dynasty (1637–1910). The initial edition of *Ŏn kandok* was in two volumes but this enlarged edition is in one. Included in the volume are thirty-seven types of letters and replies written in the Korean language, that formed a handbook of correct letter writing. There are samples of letters and replies that could be exchanged between relatives, letters of invitation and appropriate responses, and examples of correspondence marking joyful and sad occasions. Each letter provides an exemplar for addressing the envelope, as well as models for the body of the letter, and the conclusion. At the end of the book are examples of correspondence between servants and their masters. It is this last part that comprises the additional content of the enlarged edition. The book not only demonstrates how letters were crafted during this period, but is also a significant source of information for Korean linguistic history and everyday life of the period. It provides good examples of the orthography, common vocabulary, and the honorifics used in correspondence at the time. The volume is bound through five holes with white stitching. It was published by woodblock print in Ya-dong in the western part of Hanyang (currently Seoul), which was the capital city of the Chosŏn dynasty. It is part of the Korean book collection purchased in 1979 from the Harvard-Yenching Library. Most of the rare Korean books in the East Asian Library are written in Chinese. The fact that this rare book is written in Korean increases its significance.

HK

13

Cheng Yu Tung
East Asian Library

예수 성교 전서 [경성]: 문광 서원

Yesu sŏnggyo chŏnsŏ = Bible

N.T. Korean. [Kyŏngsŏng]: Mun'gwang Sŏwŏn, 1887.

This book is the first edition of a complete translation of the New Testament into Korean. Two Scottish missionaries stationed in Manchuria, John Ross (1842–1915) and John McIntyre (1837–1905), embarked on missionary activities in Korea. In 1875, they met two Koreans interested in the Gospel. The missionaries learned the Korean language from them and began translating the Bible into Korean. In the period between 1882 and 1887, they published thousands of copies of the Gospel and the whole New Testament. These Bibles and other tracts were distributed among Koreans in the Manchurian diaspora, and in the northwestern part of Korea by religious book dealers. In this way, Christianity was introduced from Manchuria into Korea. Special features of this Bible include its lack of word division, its translation into northwest Korean dialects, its four-hole binding with white stitching, in the Chinese style, in contrast to traditionally-bound Korean books which usually have five holes with red stitching. The British Foreign

Bible Society sent this copy to the University of Toronto's University College Library, in response to the campaign to rebuild the library's collections following the disastrous fire of February 14, 1890, in which all the books, with the exception of about a hundred, were destroyed. As Christianity is today one of the most widespread religions in South Korea, this book has great symbolic significance for the Korean Collection of the University of Toronto's East Asian Library. It is one of its earliest treasures.   *HK*

HUMANISM, REFORMATION, AND COUNTER-REFORMATION

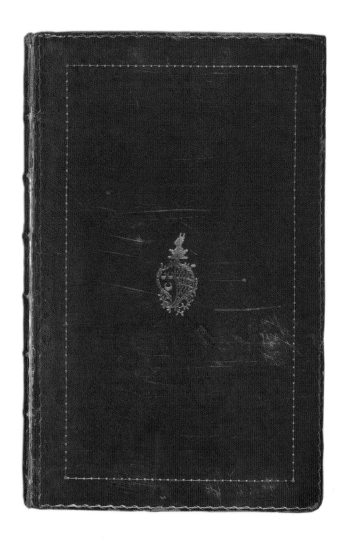

Aegidius Romanus (Giles of Rome, ca 1243–1316)
De regimine principum. [Augsburg: Günther Zainer, 27 June 1473].

An Augustinian friar and professor of theology at the University of Paris, Aegidius Romanus addressed his Latin treatise on the right conduct of kings and princes to Philip IV, known as 'the fair', who ruled France from 1285–1314. Comprising three books – on the rule of the King himself, the rule of his household, and the rule of the kingdom, *De regimine principum* was widely copied (more than three-hundred and fifty manuscripts are extant), translated into Middle English by John Trevisa, possibly as a 'mirror' for the tyrannical Richard II (who ruled from 1377 until his deposition in 1399) and later issued in several early printed editions. With the Graham Library's continuing focus on politics and international relations, it is particularly appropriate to have in the collection the first printed edition of this early work in which such topics as governance in times of both peace and war are examined philosophically. This copy is in a fine eighteenth-century russia binding with the armorial stamp and autograph notes of bibliophile Michael

Wodhull (1740–1816). It later belonged to William Morris (1834–1896) and bears the bookplate from his library at Kelmscott House, Hammersmith. Morris, who would have especially valued the folio for its elegant typography, based his own typefaces on those of the printer, Günther Zainer. The volume was in Morris's library at his death and appeared in the 1898 Sotheby's sale of his books. Gift of Guy and Sandra Upjohn in 2005, from the collection of J. Kemp Waldie.   *LC*

15

Thomas Fisher
Rare Book Library

Francesco Filelfo (1398–1481)

Francisci Philelfi satyrarum hecatostichon prima decas. Milan: Christopher Valdarfer, 1476.

This first edition of the satires of the great neo-Latin author, Francesco Filelfo, is perhaps his most enduringly significant work. A 'militant humanist', Filelfo was a towering figure in his own day, both as a scholar and a poet. By the age of thirty, he was considered the most elegant Latinist in Florence, as well as the greatest Greek scholar of his age. He was so brash and self-confident that he even satirized the reigning Medici family while still living in their city, but he was also sufficiently mercenary to eulogize the worst of the Sforzas while living in Milan. Printed in his old age, this volume preserves what Filelfo apparently considered his most enduring legacy – the satires he wrote in his middle age. They were reprinted only twice after his death: at Venice in 1502, and Paris in 1508. This first edition printing is much sought after, not only for its text, but as an example of the work of the great Milanese printer, Valdarfer, who was also responsible for the rare 1471 printing of the Boccaccio's *Decameron*. The Fisher copy also has an interesting provenance, having once been part of the Syston Park Library of Sir John Hayford Thorold, and latterly in the library of the Right Reverend John Vertue (1826–1900), first Roman Catholic Bishop of Portsmouth. *PJC*

16

CRRS, Victoria University in the University of Toronto

Lucian of Samosata (ca. 120–180)
Dialogi. Paris: Badius Ascensius, 1514.

Lucian of Samosata was a prolific and witty rhetorician who wrote in Greek, and whose works were popular with the humanists of the sixteenth century. In this text, Erasmus and Thomas More have provided a Latin translation and commentary upon a number of his satirical Dialogues. Lucian's specialty was the paradoxical encomium, and his influence appears directly in More's *Utopia*, Erasmus's *Praise of Folly*, and indirectly in the works of Leon Battista Alberti and François Rabelais. The charge of being a 'Lucianist' was often levelled at the critical and independent-minded Erasmus, the ancient author being associated with irreverence towards the gods or even atheism. More and Erasmus worked together on Lucian's works in the years 1505 and 1506, and this edition of the Dialogues is the second (the first edition being 1512). It is bound in very early wooden boards that still have their clasps intact, with scraps of a medieval manuscript on vellum. The device of the printer Josse Badius on the title page shows the operation of a printing press of the early sixteenth century.

KY

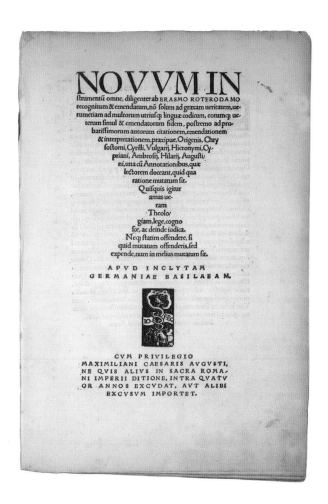

17

Bible. N.T.

Novum instrumentum. Basel: Froben, 1516.

Desiderius Erasmus of Rotterdam (1466–1536) was a tremendously influential and productive theologian and humanist scholar of the early sixteenth century. His Latin translation of the New Testament was the first new rendition of the sacred text to appear in over 1100 years since St. Jerome's Vulgate, and it was rushed through the editorial process in order to precede the Complutensian Polyglot Bible of Cardinal Jiminez which was already underway. Erasmus was deeply committed to recovering the sense of the original scriptures, and his pure and idiomatic Latin text caused a great deal of controversy by challenging the received readings of the Vulgate. He produced six editions of the Bible, the third of which provided one of the bases for the English King James edition of 1611. Although Erasmus satirized the excesses of the Church, he refused to take sides in the Reformation, hoping that scholarship would clear the air. In his preface to the New Testament, he wrote 'If the Gospel were truly preached, the Christian people would be spared many wars'. Counter-Reformation writers later accused him of having 'laid the egg that hatched the Reformation'. This first edition of Erasmus's New Testament features facing columns of Greek source texts and his Latin translation; later editions incorporated commentary and added a column for the Vulgate. It was purchased with the assistance of University of Toronto Professor Northrop Frye, who wrote *The Great Code: The Bible and Literature.* The page displayed is elegantly printed with red decoration, and marks the beginning of the letter of St. Paul to the Romans.   *KY*

18

CRRS, Victoria University in the University of Toronto

Ovid (43 B.C.E.–17 C.E.)

Metamorphosis cum luculentissimis Raphælis Regii enarrationibus. Venice: Georgius de Rusconibus, 1517.

Ovid's *Metamorphoses* is an epic pastiche of stories of transformation, one of the chief sources of the tales of Greek mythology. These stories had an enormous impact on the art and literature of the Middle Ages and Renaissance, and some, such as the tale of Narcissus, are still a part of our literary landscape. The pagan point of view, and the frequently bloody and unjust acts of sexuality and violence contained in the stories caused the *Metamorphoses* to be repeatedly subjected to allegorical commentary by Christian apologists; but in spite of the problematic content, Ovid's elegant and readable Latin also made his text a traditional teaching tool for young students. The CRRS copy is glossed by the commentary of the humanist Raphael Regius (d. 1520), who viewed Ovid as an encyclopædia of worthwhile knowledge for students, and it is accompanied by fifty-nine Italian woodcut illustrations. The displayed page demonstrates the tensions between text and interpretation, with an early reader's attempt to censor the image of the adultery of Venus and Vulcan. This book came to the CRRS collection through the 1932 bequest of Andrew James Bell, the Victoria College Professor of Classics whose library formed its nucleus and inspired the creation of the Centre for Reformation and Renaissance Studies as a research library. *KY*

19

John W. Graham Library,
Trinity College

Martin Luther (1483–1546)

Von der Freyheyt eynes Christenmenschen. Wittenberg: Melchior Lotter, 1520.

The last of the three great tracts published in the year preceding his excommunication, *The Freedom of a Christian* shows Luther at his most eloquent and remains a classic expression of the Christian faith in the

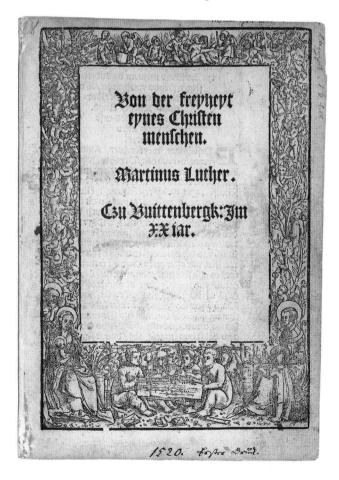

Reformation tradition. In contrast to Luther's earlier revolutionary attack on the ecclesiastical hierarchy in *The Babylonian Captivity of the Church,* this short tract has been called elevated and serene. Luther is strategically conciliatory in an accompanying dedicatory letter to Pope Leo X, yet steadfastly hostile to the institution of the papacy itself: 'Do not listen to those sirens who pretend you are no mere man but a demigod'. Luther claimed that *The Freedom of a Christian* 'contains the whole of Christian life in a brief form'. Christian liberty is rooted in the doctrine of justification by faith alone: Christ's redeeming sacrifice frees humankind from the impossible expectations of the law and good works as determinants of salvation. On the surface a paradox, Luther's seminal formulation of his doctrine of justification is famously defended in this text: 'A Christian man is the most free lord of all, and subject to none. A Christian man is the most dutiful servant of all, and subject to every one'. Good works are the natural result rather than the cause of justification. *The Freedom of a Christian* was published simultaneously in various Latin and German editions before the end of 1520. Luther's German version, though more widely influential and in substance the same, is generally considered stylistically inferior to his Latin version addressed to the Pope. Luther dedicated the German version to Hermann Mühlphordt, mayor of Zwickau, in an attempt to develop an important friendship, which would later be undermined by the Anabaptist movement. The title of this edition appears within a woodcut border attributed to Lucas Cranach. The type and ornaments had been used in the prior Leipzig edition. From the collection of J. Kemp Waldie, with his book label, this copy has a modern white pigskin binding by Sangorski and Sutcliffe, London. Gift of Guy and Sandra Upjohn in 2004.

LC

20

CRRS, Victoria University in the University of Toronto

Girolamo Savonarola (1452–1498)
Expositiones in Psalmos. Venice: Franciscus de Bindonis, 1524.

Girolamo Savonarola's life straddles the Renaissance and the Reformation. He began as an enthusiastic proponent of reform, descending on the Renaissance decadence and artistic extravagance of Medici Florence like a storm. His burning zeal won him a large number of followers, who discarded their ornaments, playing cards, books, and paintings in public 'bonfires of the vanities' during the early 1490s. For a brief period, a 'morality police' enforced a repressive regime based on spying and denunciation. Savonarola's desire for reform turned eventually upon the Church itself, and his denunciation of Pope Alexander VI earned him a summons to Rome in 1495, which he ignored, much to the Pope's annoyance. He was eventually arrested by the Florentine government, hanged, and his body was burned in May 1498. Later Protestant reformers claimed him as an early martyr for the cause of reform. The CRRS 1524 edition of Savonarola's commentary on the Psalms is an example of the small format publications that became popular during the Reformation years. This size allowed for the concealment and portability required for private devotional study. The Latin text, other than the title on the displayed page, is printed in the gothic font that was often used for works of devotion and religious significance. The woodcut illustration shows

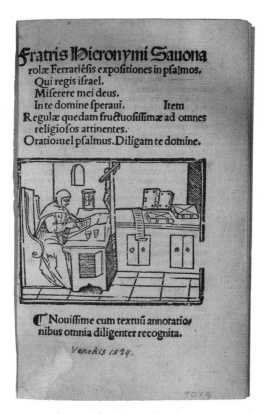

Fratris Hieronymi Sauona
rolæ Ferrariēfis expofitiones in pfalmos.
Qui regis ifrael.
Miferere mei deus.
In te domine fperaui.   Item
Regulæ quedam fruftuofiffimæ ad omnes
religiofos attinentes.
Oratio:uel pfalmus. Diligam te domine.

❡ Nouiffime cum textuū annotatio
nibus omnia diligenter recognita.
Venetiis 1524.

Savonarola at work in his study. Selections from this text were recently translated into English for the first time by University of Toronto Professor Konrad Eisenbichler in *A Guide to Righteous Living and Other Works* (Toronto: Centre for Reformation and Renaissance Studies, 2004).   KY

21

CRRS, Victoria University in the University of Toronto

Dictys Cretensis De bello Troiano libri VI [et] Daretis Phrygii De excidio Troiæ liber
Basel: Andreas Cratander, 1529.

These two early Latin texts were credited until the mid-eighteenth century to the otherwise unknown authors Dictys and Dares. They were popular because they purport to be eye-witness accounts of the Trojan War, and were considered more accurate than Homer's post-war epic, the *Iliad*. Dictys Cretensis' diary is the first-person account of a companion of Idomeneus. According to legend, his Phœnician text was discovered after an earthquake during Nero's rule. Nero had it translated into Greek, and this version, in Latin verse, was translated by Lucius Septimius in the fourth century A.D. Until 1905, when a Greek fragment on papyrus was discovered, scholars believed Septimius was the author. Dares Phrygius is mentioned by Homer as a Trojan priest of Hephæstus. His history was thought to be a fifth-century Latin translation by Cornelius Nepos because it includes a dedication to Sallust, but the language is corrupt in ways that indicate later composition. The Troy legend was diffused throughout Western Europe by these texts. Usually paired, they were translated into many languages and widely disseminated, influencing

Boccaccio, Chaucer, and Shakespeare, and were often used as textbooks. This copy from the Centre for Reformation and Renaissance Studies includes declamations by the Dutch humanist Erasmus, who took an active interest in education. This connection and its small format suggest that it was designed for study. The extensive annotations on the displayed page show the very early traces of a student's notes from a time before it was trimmed for the present vellum binding. *KY*

22
Regis College Library

Marko Marulić (1450–1524)
Euangelistarium M. Maruli Spalaten. Cologne: Hero Alopecius, 1532.

Marulić, a Croatian poet and Christian humanist, represents both the pinnacle of medieval Croatian letters as well as the birth of the Renaissance in his native land. It was his writings in Latin, however, that secured his fame throughout the rest of Europe. They were published and re-published throughout the sixteenth and seventeenth centuries, and translated into many languages. Thomas More, for example, is known to have consulted Marulić's books extensively. The *Euanglistarium* itself is a systematic discourse on ethical principles that Marulić first published in 1516. (There is some indication that the book may have appeared as early as 1487 in Reggio, but this claim has not yet been proven.) It was certainly read by Henry VIII, whose copy is annotated in the King's own hand. It has also been claimed by scholars that two of Henry's three known literary works show clear evidence of Marulić's influence. The woodcut title page is interesting for the complete lack of relationship of its ornamentation to the content of the book. An ornate frame supported by Dionysius on the right and Cleopatra being killed by the asp at the bottom, encloses the titles of the various theological and moral treatises contained within. In the eighteenth century this particular copy belonged to the Capuchin Fathers. After being acquired by the Jesuits it was located at their Guelph house and later in the library of the Toronto seminary which eventually became the Regis College Library. *PJC*

23
John M. Kelly Library,
St. Michael's College

Canones concilii provincialis Coloniensis … quibus adiectum est Encheridion Christianæ institutionis. Cologne, XXXVIII [i.e. 1538].

From the thirteenth to the eighteenth centuries, the Archbishop of Cologne was one of the seven princes who had the privilege of electing the Holy Roman Emperor. In addition to his ecclesiastical responsibilities, he was also the civil ruler of a huge territory in northwestern Germany. In 1536 the incumbent Archbishop of Cologne, Count Hermann von Wied, gathered together the bishops and other clerics of the neighbouring five dioceses in a provincial synod. The meeting was intended to clarify Church teaching on a number of points, both theological and disciplinary, and to defend the local church against increasing Protestant activity. This book includes the official decrees of the Provincial Synod of Cologne. The decrees

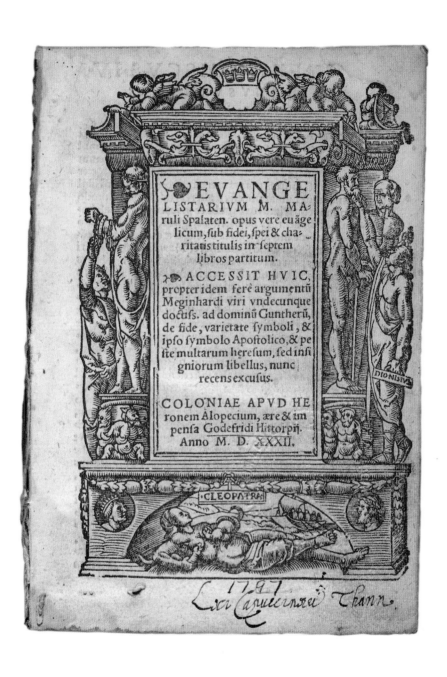

EVANGE
LISTARIVM M. MA
ruli Spalaten. opus vere euãge
licum, sub fidei, spei & cha
ritatis titulis in septem
libros partitum.

ACCESSIT HVIC,
propter idem ferè argumentũ
Meginhardi viri vndecunque
docťss. ad dominũ Guntherũ,
de fide, varietate symboli, &
ipso symbolo Apostolico, & pe
ste multarum heresum, sed insi
gniorum libellus, nunc
recens excusus.

COLONIAE APVD HE
ronem Alopecium, ære & im
pensa Godefridi Hittorpii.
Anno M. D. XXXII.

DIONISIV

CLEOPATRA

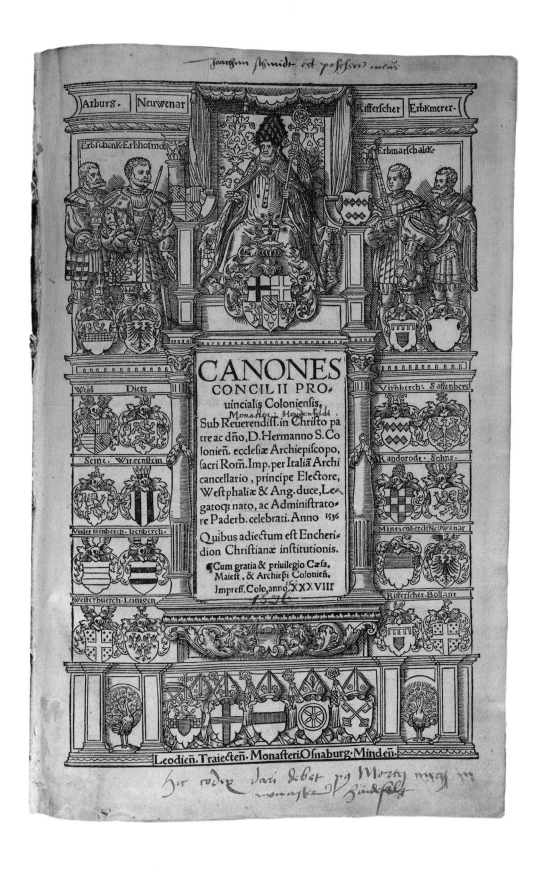

CANONES CONCILII PRO-
uincialis Coloniensis,
Sub Reuerendiss. in Christo pa
tre ac dño, D. Hermanno S. Co
lonień. ecclesiæ Archiepiscopo,
sacri Rom. Imp. per Italiã Archi
cancellario, principe Electore,
Westphaliæ & Ang. duce, Le-
gatoq; nato, ac Administrato-
re Paderb. celebrati. Anno 1536

Quibus adiectum est Encheridion Christianæ institutionis.

¶Cum gratia & priuilegio Cæsa.
Maiest. & Archiepi Colonień.
Impress. Colo. anno. XXXVIII

address a variety of topics including the administration of the sacraments, preaching, Eucharistic worship, clerical avarice, monastic life, the management of schools and hospitals, and episcopal visitations. The decrees of the synod were largely the work of one theologian, Johannes Gropper. Gropper's major theological treatise, *Enchiridion christianae institutionis*, is also included in this volume, which he wrote immediately after the synod. It begins with a clause-by-clause exposition of the Apostles' Creed, and continues with an examination of the seven sacraments and the Lord's Prayer.

Two years after the synod, Archbishop von Wied came under the influence of the Protestant reformer Martin Bucer. He tried to take his archdiocese and electorate over to Lutheranism, but was opposed by both the leading civil and ecclesiastical administrators in Cologne. In 1546 he was excommunicated by Pope Paul II, and the following year he abdicated as elector. The influence of Johannes Gropper, on the other hand, continued to increase after the Provincial Synod of Cologne. In 1541 he represented the Catholic side at the Colloquy of Regensburg, a meeting between Catholic and Protestant theologians. In 1551 he was invited to address the Council of Trent, and in 1555 he was named a cardinal by Pope Paul IV.

NM

24

CRRS, Victoria University in the University of Toronto

Niccolò Machiavelli (1469–1527)
Il principe. Venice: Comine de Trino, 1541.

The name of Niccolò Machiavelli is the source of the modern adjective 'Machiavellian', with all of its connotations of cynicism, deviousness, and political brinksmanship. His 1513 work *The Prince* is an outline of the characteristics required for the effective ruler, and is said to be based upon the real-life example of

Cesare Borgia. It was revolutionary for its time because it separated good rule from piety: the good ruler is someone who risks everything even the damnation of his very soul, for the sake of stable government. Some readers have assumed that the text is a satire whose actual purpose is to expose tyranny and promote republican government because of the delight that Machiavelli seems to take in scorning convention. This CRRS edition is printed in italic type and displays a woodcut portrait of the author, labelled N.M.   *KY*

25

CRRS, Victoria University in the University of Toronto

Martin Luther (1483–1546)

Hausspostille. Nuremburg: Valentin Geissler, 1565.

Martin Luther is generally recognized as the father of the Protestant Reformation. The 'Hausspostille' (house-sermons) were originally preached between 1530 and 1534, and first published in 1544. Luther was assisted in this work by his secretary Veit Dietrich (1506–1549), and Georg Rörer (1492–1557), a note-taker who transcribed his sermons as Luther gave them, without notes, after meditation, in the inspiration of the moment. The sermons are arranged according to the seasons of the Catholic Church calendar. Most of Luther's sermons are accompanied by woodcut illustrations, each of which has been hand-coloured in this copy by an early reader. The illustration displayed, for the sixth Sunday after Epiphany, shows the parable of the wheat and the tares, in which a landowner's enemy (inspired by the devil) sows weeds among his wheat. The illustration is interesting for its use of contemporary clothing and architecture. *KY*

26

Regis College Library

Bartolomeo Platina (1421–1481)

Historia B. Platinæ de vitis pontificum Romanorum. Cologne: Maternus Cholinus, 1574.

Platina was born in Piadena near Mantua, Italy and died in his sixtieth year in Rome. A humanist, he was for a time imprisoned on suspicion of heresy and of conspiring against the life of the Pope, though the latter charge was dropped for lack of evidence, and he was eventually acquitted of the former charge. Having been rejected by Pope Paul II (1417–1471), Platina exacted his revenge on the pontiff by writing this book at the suggestion of Pope Sixtus IV (1414–1484). In it he paints Paul as a cruel tyrant, and an archenemy of science. For centuries this book influenced historical opinion on Paul until recent critical re-evaluations of the sources have proven that many of Platina's characterizations were biased and inaccurate. *De vitis pontificum*, however, remains a significant text since it marks the first effort at creating a systematic handbook of papal history.   *PJC*

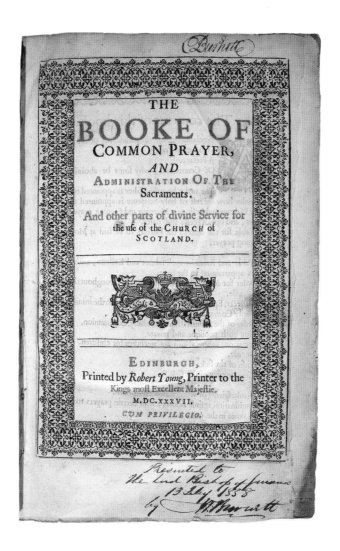

27

The Booke of Common Prayer, and Administration Of The Sacraments. And other Parts of Divine Service for the use of the Church of Scotland. Edinburgh: Printed by Robert Young, 1637.

Famously known as 'the Scottish Prayer Book', the 1637 Book of Common Prayer represents an attempt during the reign of Charles I (some say, the first step on the road to the scaffold) to bring Scottish practice into conformity with the form of public worship prescribed in the English Prayer Book of 1559, which had never been adopted by the Scots. The 1637 BCP was in fact the work of Scottish bishops, notably John Maxwell, Bishop of Ross, and James Wedderburn, Bishop of Dunblane, not the English Archbishop Laud, to whom it was widely credited, and it included several elements meant to appeal to the Scots, such as use of the word 'presbyter' rather than 'priest' and a Communion service based on the earlier English BCP from 1549. Its scriptural passages, including the Psalms, were taken from the new King James Version of the Bible. Whatever its merits, the book was doomed from the start by a failure to undertake what would now be called the necessary 'consensus-building'. Lacking prior approval of the General Assembly of the

Scottish Church, the Royal Proclamation directing every parish to procure at least two copies provoked a legendary event recounted by Wycliffe College's Professor Dyson Hague: 'When the Dean opened the Book to begin the service on that 23rd day of July, 1637, in the Cathedral Church in Edinburgh, a riot started. An old woman [one Jenny Geddes, who had a stall in the High Street] … picked up a stool and hurled it at the Dean's head, and the Bishop and the Dean, ignominiously retreating, escaped only with their lives.' Rejected in Scotland in spite of its intrinsic merits, the never-used 1637 Prayer Book nonetheless has had significant lasting influence on American Prayer Books from 1789 to the present and on later revisions of the English BCP. Now a part of the Graham Library's extensive collection of versions of the Book of Common Prayer used in Anglican churches throughout the world for the past four and a half centuries, this book, which is bound with both Edinburgh and London Psalters dated 1636, was a gift to the Trinity College Library from Hugh Anson-Cartwright in 1996.   *LC*

28

John W. Graham Library, Trinity College

Richard Hooker (1554–1600)
The Works of Mr. Richard Hooker … Vindicating the Church of England as truly Christian, and duly Reformed: In Eight Books of Ecclesiastical Polity. Now compleated … With an account of his Holy Life, and Happy Death, Written by Dr. John Gauden. London: Printed by J. Best, for Andrew Crook, 1662.

The 'judicious' Richard Hooker has been deemed not only defender, but inventor of 'Anglicanism'. His *Of the Lawes of Ecclesiasticall Politie* is not only the founding theological text for the study of the English church, with its own specific doctrine, discipline, and mission, but arguably 'the first major work in the fields of theology, philosophy, and political thought to be written in English' (DNB). In 1662 John Gauden, Bishop of Exeter, edited this new folio of Hooker's works, the first to include all eight books of the *Lawes.* The first four books were first published in 1593 and the fifth in 1597. The sixth and eighth books were printed separately in 1648 and the seventh uncovered in manuscript and first printed in this edition. Gauden also provided a highly inaccurate *Life* of Hooker and, as a frontispiece, an engraved portrait by Faithorne which was a conventionalized likeness based on the effigy put up over Hooker's tomb thirty-five years after his death. The engraved title by William Hole had appeared in prior folio editions from 1611 to 1623. The Gauden edition, with its claim of authenticity for the three posthumous books, was an embarrassment to many of the Restoration episcopate and provoked Izaak Walton's famous *Life* of 1665, which corrected Gauden's biography and attempted to discredit the later books. This 1662 folio was acquired by the Graham Library in 2004 as part of the collection belonging to W. Speed Hill, general editor of *The Folger Library Edition of the Works of Richard Hooker* (1977–1998), through the generosity of W. Speed Hill and David and Mary Neelands.   *LC*

SVNT MELIORA MIHI.

RICHARDVS HOOKER *Exoniensis scholaris*
sociusq; Collegij Corp: Christi Oxon: deinde Londi:
Templi interioris in Sacris magister Rectorq;
huius Ecclesiæ, scripsit octo libros Politiæ
Ecclesiasticæ Anglicanæ, quorum tres desi:
derantur. Obijt An: Do̅: M.DC.III. Ætat:
suæ L.
Posuit hoc pijssimo viro monumentum An̅o
Do̅: M.DC.XXX.V. Guli: Cowper Armiger,
in Christo Iesu quem genuit per Evangelium.
1.ᵃ Corinth: 4. 15.

Guil. Faithorne sculp.

51

29

Regis College Library

Mathias Tanner (1630–1692)

Societas Jesu usque ad sanguinis et vitæ profusionem militans, in Europa, Africa, Asia, et America, contra gentiles, Mahometanos, Judæos, hæreticos, impios, pro Deo fide, Ecclesia, pietate; sive, Vita, et mors eorum, qui ex Societate Jesu in causa fidei, & virtutis propugnatæ, violentâ morte toto orbe sublati sunt. Prague: Typis Universitatis Carolo-Ferdinandeæ, 1675.

Mathias Tanner was a native of Pilsen in Bohemia. He entered the Jesuit order in 1646 and remained most of his life in Prague where he was successively a teacher, rector of the imperial university, and superior of the Bohemian province of the Society of Jesus. He wrote four books, two of which (including this compendium of biographies) dealt with the labours, suffering, and martyrdoms of the members of his order. Each biography is illustrated with an often graphic engraved vignette in a characteristic Bohemian baroque style. The work is arranged in four parts: Europe, Africa, Asia, America, with the longest section devoted to Asia.   *PJC*

52

THEOLOGY AND SPIRITUALITY

30

The Ardagh Chalice (Ireland, 8th century).

Ranking with the *Book of Kells* as one of the finest known works of Celtic art, the Ardagh Chalice is a two-handled silver cup decorated with gold, gilt bronze, brass, lead pewter and enamel, and is assembled from three-hundred and fifty-four separate pieces. It is encircled by inset gold wirework panels of animals, birds, and geometric interlace. Techniques used in its fabrication include hammering, engraving, lost-wax casting, filigree appliqué, cloisonné and enamelling. It was probably intended for use at the altar, since it bears the names of the apostles incised in a frieze around the bowl. The chalice was first unearthed in 1847, then lost by children playing with it, and was then found again in 1868 by two boys digging in a potato field near the village of Ardagh, County Limerick. It currently resides in the National Museum of Ireland. This unique replica was made by the artist-craftsman who restored the original. After display at the World's Fair in St. Louis in 1904, it was acquired by the Canadian Senator Charles Murphy, who bequeathed it to the Pontifical Institute of Mediaeval Studies in 1935.   *JF*

31

Greek Manuscript leaf on vellum (10th century).

The leaf shown here is the oldest sample in the Institute's collection acquired to instruct students in palaeography. It originally belonged to a tenth-century book of homilies written in brown and red ink (as on the verso of this leaf). The text of this leaf contains a solemn exhortation, or curse, against vermin that infest a farm or garden. It is usually attributed to Saint Trypho, the patron saint of gardeners. It reads (in part):

> In the name of the Father and of the Son and of the Holy Ghost. ... Go forth from this vineyard and from this farm and garden, ... you ground creepers, ... milliped worms, locusts, ... grasshoppers, macrochoppers, snails, ... which go into the branches of the vineyard and garden and the fruit of the grape bunches.... I command you by oath: beware of this oath and go forth from this vineyard, this garden, and this farm, and do not harm the fruit in this place, but withdraw to the wild hills and the trees which do not bear fruit, for there the Lord has given you your daily food...' (Translation anonymous)   *JF*

32

Gratian (12th century)
Decretum aureum divi Gratiani, in quo est discordantium canonum concordia. Paris: Ulrich Gering and Berchtold Rembolt, 1501.

In the twelfth century, the expanding, centralized Church in Rome needed a comprehensive system of law and discipline to replace the hodgepodge of rulings and decisions that had been decreed over hundreds of years. In 1140 a jurist in Bologna named Gratian, drawing on about four thousand texts from

early theologians, church councils, and papal rulings over several centuries, applied the new scholastic method popularized by Peter Abelard to reconcile the contradictions and discrepancies of those past texts into a logical and practical presentation of Church law, organization, and discipline. In one hundred and one 'distinctions' and thirty-six 'causes,' to which he later added elements drawn from Roman civil law, he arrived at a 'Harmony of Discordant Canons' that became popularly known as the *Decretum.* Later jurists like Johannes Teutonicus (ca. 1218) commented on Gratian's text, and a revision of Teutonicus by Bartolomeo da Brescia (ca.1245) became the standard presentation of the *Decretum* that was copied in hundreds of manuscripts. Gratian's *Decretum* and its commentaries, updated by later collections like the *Decretales* and *Extravagantes,* remained the basis of canon law until the early twentieth century. As shown in this Paris 1501 edition, early printed editions retained the manuscript tradition of placing the text of the *Decretum* in the centre of the page and surrounding it with the later commentaries, or 'glosses,' on the text, in smaller print.

JF

33

*Pontifical Institute
of Mediaeval Studies*

Missale secundum ordinem Carthusiensium

Ed. Johannes Binchois. Lyon: Simon Bevilaqua, 9 May 1517.

The production of missals to accommodate the celebration of Mass in thousands of European churches and monasteries accounted for a large percentage of early printed books. The missal shown here was printed for the use of the Carthusian Order, which at the time had hundreds of monasteries in western Europe. This copy belonged to the Carthusian monastery of Maria Saal (founded 1402) at Buxheim, near Memmingen, in Germany. In addition to the 'ordinary texts' of the Mass and the 'proper' prayers needed for each Sunday and principal feasts throughout the year, this missal includes the epistles and gospels read on each occasion. There is also a liturgical calendar that shows the feasts of Christ and the saints for each day of each month, as well as 'commons' for Masses of the several categories of saints and prayers prescribed for various needs and occasions.

This copy has manuscript paste-ins and some manuscript notations in the margins. At the head of the book stands a hand-coloured woodcut, framed in gold leaf, representing Saint Bruno, the founder of the Carthusian order. The full-page woodcut shown here, facing folio 1, represents God the Father enthroned and surrounded by the symbols of the four evangelists. A full-page woodcut of the crucifixion of Christ, with Mary and Saint John at the foot of the cross, hand-coloured in green, blue, orange, brown, yellow, beige, and gold leaf, is placed at the head of the 'Canon' – the central and most solemn part – of the Mass. There are two hundred and seventy-three hand-coloured historiated initials. Musical notations have been introduced by hand on printed red staves. The binding is contemporary blind-stamped vellum over wooden boards. It lacks the brass corner pieces, centre ornament, and clasps that originally adorned and protected the book. *JF*

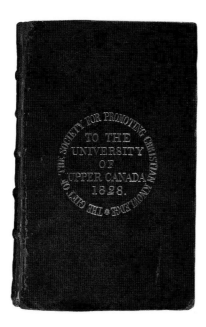

34

John W. Graham Library,
Trinity College

Catechismvs Romanvs, Ex Decreto Concilii Tridentini, & Pii. V. Pontificis Maximi jussu primum editus … Andreæ Fabricii Leodii. Antwerp: Plantin, 1596.

This Roman Catechism is one of some four hundred theological books secured by John Strachan in 1828 as a gift from the Church of England's Society for Promoting Christian Knowledge to stock the shelves of his projected Church university in Upper Canada, an institution which finally opened as the University of King's College in 1843 and became the University of Toronto in 1850, 'secularized' at that time by the provincial Legislative Assembly. The elderly Bishop Strachan, having resigned as president of King's

College, then proceeded to raise the funds and inspire the necessary support to found the University of Trinity College in 1852 as an institution that would uphold his original ideals. The authorities of the 'godless' University of Toronto were soon persuaded to return these books to their 'rightful home', where they remain to this day as the SPCK Collection at the heart of Trinity College's special collections supporting studies in Anglican theology and church history. All the volumes in this collection – notably, the first collection acquired for what is now the University of Toronto Library – bear the donor's gilt stamp on their front boards: 'The Gift of the Society for Promoting Christian Knowledge to the University of Upper Canada 1828'.

LC

35

Regis College Library

St. Robert Bellarmine (1542–1621)

Explanatio in Psalmos. Lyon: H. Cardon, 1611.

Bellarmine, a distinguished Jesuit theologian, writer, and cardinal, studied and taught at some of the finest Catholic universities of Counter-Reformation Europe. Educated for the priesthood in Rome, he continued his theological studies in Padua and Louvain. He rapidly gained a reputation for excellence in confronting the Protestant controversialists of his day, and in 1597 was appointed chief theologian to the papal household, Examiner of Bishops, and Consultor of the Holy Office. This text, however, represents the fine scholarly and exegetical mind that Bellarmine possessed. Printed at Lyons in 1611, this book was considered by far the best Catholic commentary on the Psalms until the twentieth century. Bellarmine had actually mastered Hebrew, and was thus able to apply the scientific and linguistic methods of textual criticism, comparing and interpreting the Hebrew and Vulgate versions of the text. On occasion, he lets tradition trump erudition, preferring the less accurate renderings of the latter over the purity of the former.   *PJC*

36

John W. Graham Library,
Trinity College

Jakob Böhme (1575–1624)

The Works of Jacob Behmen, the Teutonic Theosopher…With Figures, Illustrating His Principles, Left by the Reverend William Law. London: Printed for M. Richardson, 1764–1781.

The writings of the German mystic, Jacob Böhme (or Behmen in England) had a profound influence on both William Law (1686–1761), known mainly for his early spiritual classic, *A Serious Call to a Devout and Holy Life* (1729), and the visionary artist and poet, William Blake (1757–1827), who in 1825 said of the illustrations in this edition: 'Michelangelo could not have done better'. Law's focus on humanity's fallen state and the subsequent regeneration of the soul through the Christian faith is reflected in the elaborate paper engineering in this English edition of Behmen. 'Inward Man is alone the Subject of Religion and divine Grace,' Law wrote. These illustrations, which Law is credited with preserving, use layers of paper flaps, a technique dating back to the fourteenth century for anatomical illustrations, to depict metaphorically the inward states of the soul in relation to the body. Of the 'Three Tables of Divine Revelation' the First represents Man before his fall, in purity, dominion, and glory; the Second after his fall, in pollution and perdition; the Third rising from his fall to his last perfection. Flaps or 'Vails' in the Third Table, shown here, progressively reveal the movement of the soul from the beginning of regeneration to redemption; from the setting of a wilderness landscape outside the city of London, with St. Paul's Cathedral in the background, to an ordered garden; from male to female. The illustrations are the work of an anonymous London engraver after drawings by the German artist J.C. Leuchter, which were in turn based on diagrams by the compiler, Dionysius Andreas Freyer. Gift to the Trinity College Library from Sir Edmund Osler, M.P., 1913.   *LC*

Ian, as to all his
e: But it can-
ſerved in the
Three together
erefore is here
bſervations are
r Part of him,
ng; Secondly,
egeneration be

oft Repreſenta
ch before in
Immortal
which
ence.—
of it
l as t
ginnin
with
was
was
decla
d of
Spir
preſe
n the
ible H
is the 1
notes
ble. An
nd abou
ut any Be
them narrow
ch forth them-
But this ſame
all illuminate
oſs and thick
d, true, real,
God, moving
t Light of the
It is then a
t forth the firſt
evertheleſs not
, Day by Day,
one Side, is a
ſpelling of the

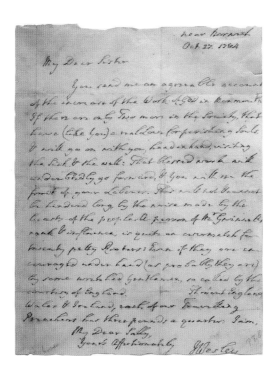

37

United Church Archives-
Victoria University Archives

John Wesley (1703–1791)
Autograph Letter Signed to Miss Sally Baker, 27 October 1784.

John Wesley, scholar, preacher, educator, churchman, and general superintendent of the Methodist movement, was born on June 28, 1703 at Epworth, England. He entered Christ Church College, Oxford in 1720; was ordained deacon and priest in the Church of England in 1725 and 1728 respectively. In 1726, he was elected a Fellow of Lincoln College where he lectured in Greek and New Testament Studies, and began publishing in 1733. Wesley accepted a chaplaincy in the Colony of Georgia in 1735, a mission lasting less than two years. On May 24, 1738, he had a major conversion experience at Aldersgate in London which renewed his trust in personal salvation. His study of Moravian and Arminian theology, as well as the Bible and the Church Fathers, further strengthened this trust. In 1739, Wesley began what became a Methodist hallmark – field preaching. Many Church of England churches were closed to Methodist preachers so Wesley followed George Whitefield's example and preached to the miners out of doors near Bristol. For fifty years he preached throughout Great Britain in chapels, collieries, and farmer's fields, stirring an unimagined religious revival. In 1744, he organized the first annual conference to forge strategy and establish a discipline for the Methodist Society. Over his long career, Wesley published hundreds of volumes of sermons, correspondence, journals, hymns, and church services; edited the *Arminian Magazine* from 1778 until his death; and wrote on historical, literary, scientific, and theological topics. At age eighty-six on February 23, 1791, he preached his last sermon in Kent, and died on March 2 of the same year. The John Wesley papers at the Archives include correspondence, both original and in facsimile, of Wesley to his family and associates.   *SR*

38

Ne yakawea yondereanayendaghkwa oghseragwegouh, neoni yakawea ne orighwadogeaghty yondatnekosseraghs, neoni tekarighwagehhadont. London: Karistodarho C. Buckton, 1787.

While this book is the fourth Mohawk edition of the Book of Common Prayer, it also represents the first appearance of any complete biblical text printed in that aboriginal language. Joseph Brant (1742–1807) completed this translation of the Gospel of St. Mark in 1774, while he was working under the direction of John Stuart, of the Society for the Propagation of the Gospel at Fort Hunter in the old colony of New York. In 1781 Daniel Claus, an Indian interpreter and lieutenant in the Royal American Regiment, transported Brant's manuscript to England, and saw it incorporated into the Prayer Book at the expense of the British Government. The volume also includes nineteen engravings executed by James Peachey (d. 1797). Peachey had been a surveyor, draughtsman, army officer, and artist who had worked throughout the British colonies in North America both before and after the American Revolution. As this book demonstrates, he also tried his hand at book illustration through an association with the London printer Christopher Buckton. In 1786 he etched the frontispiece to Claus's *A Primer for the Use of the Mohawk Children*, and in the following year he illustrated this volume. Peachey eventually returned to Canada where he executed portraits of Joseph Brant and his wife Catherine. This book is now part of the Knox College collection of rare books on deposit at the Thomas Fisher Rare Book Library. *PJC*

FRONTISPIECE

Christian Guardian
Toronto: The Methodist Church, 1829–1925.

The role of the Methodist press in nineteenth-century Canada was significant enough that in 1894 it actually had few competitors. J. Macdonald Oxley, a businessman and writer, mentioned that 'the press is the most powerful factor in modern affairs'. It is widely known that some religious publications were directed to a wide general readership – especially the *Christian Guardian*. The first issue of the *Christian Guardian* appeared on November 21, 1829. It was published in a building located on March St., Toronto, north of the new Court House, and started with a total circulation of five hundred. Within three years it had reached three thousand, the largest circulation of any periodical, religious or secular in Canada at that time. This weekly newspaper was the organ of the Wesleyan Methodists. It had a tremendous influence among all non-Conformists, pursuing a middle of the road path politically. Although violently opposed to the privileges of the Church of England, it otherwise supported the conservative cause. Lord Sydenham called it 'the only decent paper in both Canadas'. Its most famous editor was Egerton Ryerson, who edited it from 1829–1832, 1833–1835, and 1838–1840. Before Confederation, it was also edited by Rev. James Richardson, Ephraim Evans, Rev. Jonathan Scott, Rev. George Frederick Playter, Rev. George R. Sanderson, Rev. James Spencer, and Rev. Wellington Jeffers. *The New Outlook* absorbed the *Guardian* in 1925.   *SR*

James Evans (1801–1846)
The Cree Syllabic Hymn Book. Norway House: Printed by James Evans, 1841.

41   James Evans
'Cree syllabic system,' printed proof created by Evans using a press that arrived at Norway House, Manitoba in 1842.

42   Samples of Evans's Cree Syllabic Alphabet Type: Three type slugs cast by Evans, ca. 1840.

Unique in the annals of Canadian typography, this western Canadian 'incunable' was printed in 1841 by the Rev. James Evans at Norway House, Hudson's Bay Territory (Manitoba), on a modified press used for packing animal pelts. James Evans was a Methodist minister who was appointed superintendent of missions in the Hudson's Bay Company territories by the Methodist Missionary Society in Britain. He was an author, a translator and the developer of the Cree syllabary. Evans devised this 'alphabet' to transliterate the Cree language as a script. His motivation was to further the spread of Christian literature. The Cree syllabic system was based on a pattern of thirty-six rotating shapes grouped in nine basic characters and

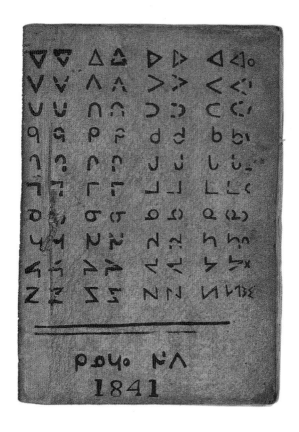

placed facing four different directions to indicate different vowels to express elementary syllabic sounds. James Evans used his penknife to whittle oak type moulds of the Cree alphabet, cast the type by melting down bullets and lead from the lining of tea-chests, and made ink from chimney soot. As it was easy to learn, the Cree syllabic system was enormously successful with the Cree people. Within a short time, nearly the whole Cree community was able to read using the syllabics and James Evans became known as 'the man who made birch bark talk.' The Cree syllabic system continues to be in use among aboriginal communities in Canada and the northern United States today. Victoria University Library owns the only three recorded copies of Evans' 1841 hymn book. The text of all three is identical, but there are slight differences in paper, binding, and cover. The display item, for example, is bound in elk skin. All are printed on coarse paper. Evans' *Cree Syllabic Hymn Book* is of significant interest to researchers of native North American history. The three hymn books were acquired in 1910 from Miss Sophia Evans, niece of James Evans. Dr. John Maclean, missionary, book collector, and author, obtained James Evans' Cree syllabic type at Norway House in 1925. Earlier provenance of the type is unknown. They were acquired from Maclean in 1940, along with two boxes of modern Cree syllabic type. GZ

43

United Church Archives-
Victoria University Archives

Canadian Methodist Magazine
Toronto: Methodist Book-Room, 1875–1888.

Methodism and the printed word have a particularly historic relationship, rooted in the theology of John Wesley. It was known that Wesley expected his preachers to spend at least five hours every morning reading. In 1874 the first General Conference of the newly formed Methodist Church of Canada recommended that a 'good monthly magazine' should be published. Following the Conference, a magazine with a significant amount of reading material was born. The *Canadian Methodist Magazine* introduced a specific kind of religious journalism to nineteenth-century Canada, by embracing topics of both religion and science. The copy displayed contains annotations of William Henry Withrow who was editor of the magazine.

SR

44

John M. Kelly Library,
St. Michael's College

John Henry Cardinal Newman (1801–1890)
A Letter Addressed to His Grace the Duke of Norfolk, on Occasion of Mr. Gladstone's Recent Expostulation. London: B.M. Pickering, 1875.

This copy of the first edition John Henry Cardinal Newman's text is particularly notable for its autograph by the author and the letter with which it is bound. Both are addressed to Sir George Bowyer, Bt. (1811–1883), a legal scholar, Member of Parliament, and another English Catholic convert of the nineteenth century. The letter is significant as it shows the connection between two of nineteenth-century England's best known Catholic apologists. After Bowyer's conversion in 1850, he became a prominent lay defender of the Catholic Church, writing particularly in favour of the new Catholic Episcopal hierarchy of England and against the seizure of papal land in Italy (often in response to the British Prime Minister Lord Palmerston). Through the letter, we see a personal and professional connection of two leading figures who fought against the tide in Victorian England to defend their newly-adopted faith. In the publication itself, Newman responds to William Ewart Gladstone's pamphlet *The Vatican Decrees in their Bearing on Civil Allegiance.* Here, the four-time Prime Minister of Great Britain and prominent Anglican asserted that those who believed in the doctrine of papal infallibility were not loyal citizens. Newman's response was one of many replies by Catholics to the pamphlet.

DS

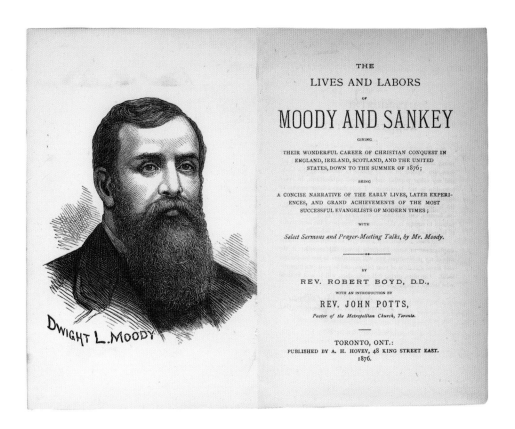

THE

LIVES AND LABORS

OF

MOODY AND SANKEY

GIVING

THEIR WONDERFUL CAREER OF CHRISTIAN CONQUEST IN
ENGLAND, IRELAND, SCOTLAND, AND THE UNITED
STATES, DOWN TO THE SUMMER OF 1876;

BEING

A CONCISE NARRATIVE OF THE EARLY LIVES, LATER EXPERI-
ENCES, AND GRAND ACHIEVEMENTS OF THE MOST
SUCCESSFUL EVANGELISTS OF MODERN TIMES;

WITH

Select Sermons and Prayer-Meeting Talks, by Mr. Moody.

BY

REV. ROBERT BOYD, D.D.,

WITH AN INTRODUCTION BY

REV. JOHN POTTS,

Pastor of the Metropolitan Church, Toronto.

TORONTO, ONT.:
PUBLISHED BY A. H. HOVEY, 48 KING STREET EAST.
1876.

DWIGHT L. MOODY

45

United Church Archives-
Victoria University Archives

Robert Boyd

The Lives and Labors of Moody and Sankey. Toronto: A.H. Hovey, 1876.

In addition to journals, the Methodist press issued many edifying books, celebrating the evangelical activities of missionaries like Dwight Lyman Moody (1837–1899) and Ira David Sankey (1840–1908). Moody was born in Northfield, Massachusetts, converted in 1855, and joined a Congregational Church the following year. While working with the Chicago Young Men's Christian Association, Moody developed his skills as a speaker. Sankey, a native of Edinburgh, Pennsylvania, was a lifelong Methodist with a remarkable voice which he used to 'sing the gospel'. The two met at a YMCA conference in 1870 and joined forces in several evangelical tours on both sides of the Atlantic, commencing with the highly successful tour of Britain in 1873–1875. The publishing era following the American Civil War, particularly the period 1878–1889, is often designated 'The Gilded Age' because gilt ornament became more common as bookbinders moved from leather to cloth for the covering of books. During the 1850s, the typical book issued by the Methodist Book Concern was bound in dark brown or black muslin, blind-stamped with scrollwork and medallions on the front and back of the case, and heavily gilded on the spine. These trends continued during the 1860s, gradually moving toward a more delicate design.   S R

46   Architectural Drawing for the Methodist Publishing House. [Toronto, 1913–1914]

United Church Archives-
Victoria University Archives

The first Methodist Book Room was built in 1829 on March Street (now Lombard), Toronto near the Court House. In 1834 it relocated to Toronto Street near the old jail for four years. Five years later, a brick building was erected on King Street facing Government House. Egerton Ryerson became editor and his brother John Ryerson became book steward of the new premises. In 1889, the old Richmond Street Church was remodeled, with part of the building being used for the Publishing House and part for the offices of the parish itself. After many extensions and alterations the building was deemed inadequate for the Church's needs. In 1912 the property on the corner of Queen and John Streets was purchased for $210,000 and a purpose-built structure was erected in 1913–1914. The Publishing House and the Church Offices were moved to it in 1915 and the Wesley Building, as it was known, became the headquarters of the Methodist Church and subsequently the United Church of Canada. It also served as the plant for the Methodist Publishing Company and its successor, the Ryerson Press. In 1959 the United Church headquarters moved to 85 St. Clair Avenue East in Toronto, and in 1971 the Ryerson Press was sold. The Wesley Building is now the headquarters for CITY-TV. *SR*

47
United Church Archives-
Victoria University Archives

John Maclean (1851–1928)
Manuscript diary, June 1919.

John Maclean was a Methodist minister, historian, and missionary. Born in Scotland, he obtained his doctoral degree in history from Wesleyan University, Bloomington, Illinois (1888) after finishing his degree (M.A. in theology) at Victoria University, Cobourg (1887). In 1926, at the age of 75, he received a degree in law (LL.B.) from the University of Manitoba. He was a missionary to native peoples in the Canadian North West and Ontario. He edited *The Wesleyan* from 1902 to 1906, and worked as archivist of the Methodist Church and librarian of Wesley College, Winnipeg from 1918 to 1928. He studied native culture, and wrote several books chiefly on aboriginal peoples, including a *Life of James Evans* (whose Cree hymn book and original type pieces are also in this exhibition), *The Indians of Canada*, and a *Grammar of the Blackfoot Language*, as well as a large number of pamphlets, papers and tracts on scientific and religious subjects. The John Maclean papers at the Archives include correspondence with scholars of native languages and history, diaries and notebooks, manuscripts, typescripts, notes of histories, devotional works, fiction, memorabilia, and other personal material, marriage stubs, clippings, and personal corre-spondence. *SR*

48
United Church Archives-
Victoria University Archives

Katharine B. Hockin (1910–1993)
Signed typed form letter addressed to Mary, 4 September 1941.

Katharine Hockin was a missionary, teacher, author, and administrator during her long ministry within the United Church of Canada. She was born in China of missionary parents Arthur Hockin Jr. and his wife Lily. Katharine obtained a doctorate in education from Columbia University (1948), and a Bachelor of Divinity from Serampore University, Calcutta (1961). She also received an honorary LL.D. degree from Mount Allison University, and an honorary Doctor of Divinity degree from Victoria University in 1977. Hockin began her missionary work in 1937 as Maritime secretary of the Student Christian Movement in Canada. She was commissioned as a missionary to China by the Maritime Conference in 1939, and remained there until 1952, working in various positions for the Women's Missionary Society. She taught at the United Church Training School in Toronto after she returned from the Chinese mission (1952–1958)

and from 1960–1964, she was World Mission Visitor for SCM. In 1964 she became Dean of Students at the Canadian School of Missions and Ecumenical Institute. From 1973 until her retirement in 1976 she served as Interim Director of the School. She also served on several committees of the United Church of Canada, particularly within the Division of World Outreach. The Katherine B. Hockin papers at the Archives are part of the Hockin family papers and include student records, correspondence, notes, teaching materials, writings, reports, notes on China, newspaper clippings, and diaries of trips to China.   *SR*

49

*United Church Archives-
Victoria University Archives*

The Holy Bible: containing the Old and New Testaments Translated out of the Original Tongues and with the Former Translations Diligently Compared and Revised by His Majesty's Special Command: Appointed to be Read in Churches: authorized King James Version. London: Oxford University Press, Printed by the Ryerson Press (Canada), 1943–1944.

As the special title page to this book declares, this was the first copy of the Authorized Version of the Bible actually printed and bound in Canada. In 1943, the Rev. C.H. Dickinson, book steward for the United Church Publishing House, noted that there were problems emerging in the book trade because of the war. A shortage of staff, the increased cost of goods and services, the scarcity of materials and merchandise

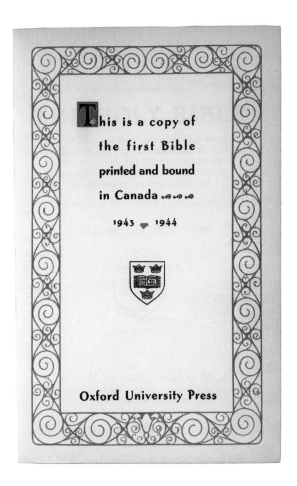

This is a copy of
the first Bible
printed and bound
in Canada ෴ ෴ ෴
1943 ⬥ 1944

Oxford University Press

were all being felt, and both the reading public and publishers were turning more to home-grown products. In April of the following year Dickinson reported to the United Church Board of Publication that 'during the present year it may well be increasingly difficult to obtain books from the United States as well as from Great Britain. This may tend to stimulate another good season for Canadian books'. One lucrative enterprise that emerged as a result of such privation was the first appearance of a Canadian King James Bible, which up to that time been printed and bound only in England and then shipped for sale and distribution throughout the rest of the Empire. Although the copyright for the Bible was technically vested in the King as a result of his coronation oath, practically speaking the King's Printer, Eyre and Spottiswoode, held the rights of publication, together with Oxford and Cambridge upon whom the privilege had devolved. The difficulties of the war, however, had made access to paper and ink difficult, and so the project was contracted out in Canada to the United Church Publishing House which published an initial run of 30,000 copies, from British plates made in 1943 and imported the following year. The publication of the Authorized Version of the Bible has remained in Canada ever since. *PJC*

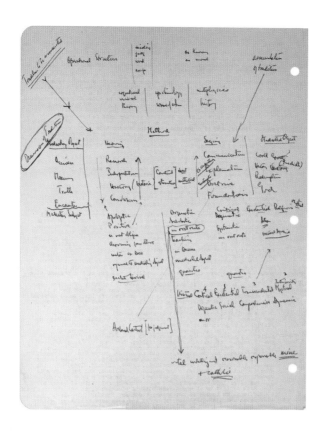

50

Bernard Lonergan Archives,
Lonergan Research Institute

Bernard J. F. Lonergan (1904–1984)
Pages from Insight Typescript, [s.d., ca. 1951 or 1952].

These pages are taken from one of Lonergan's early typescripts of chapter 1 of his first great book, *Insight: A Study of Human Understanding*. Lonergan once said that he would write and rewrite individual pages some twenty times before he was satisfied. His personal papers are filled with illustrations of the care with which he wrote. The Lonergan archives contain several other attempts at precisely this same material.

RD

51

Bernard Lonergan Archives,
Lonergan Research Institute

Bernard J. F. Lonergan
Page from Lonergan Archives. Manuscript, 1965.

The significace of this page lies in the fact that it represents probably the first written record of Lonergan's 1965 insight into the structure of the discipline of theology. In the view of his students, Lonergan has definitively mapped theology into eight operational or functional specialties: research, interpretation, history, dialectic, foundations, doctrines, systematics, and communications. This page shows his first recorded statement of that division. Some of the terms are different, but the basic conception is recorded here. The page will provide the editors of the *Collected Works* with a frontispiece for the critical edition of *Method in Theology*.

RD

52

Bernard Lonergan Archives,
Lonergan Research Institute

R.G. Collingwood. (1889–1943)
The Idea of History. New York: Oxford University Press, 1972.

Bernard Lonergan's personal copy of R.G. Collingwood's important book *The Idea of History* was found in his possession after his death. The sidelining in the book is Lonergan's typical manner of indicating passages that caught his attention. In *Insight* Lonergan proposed a cognitional theory that he illustrated in mathematics, natural science, philosophy, and theology. But he had not yet applied his cognitional theory to historical scholarship. That is one of the major accomplishments of his next great book, *Method in Theology*. Collingwood was one of the authors who helped him in this regard. In *Method in Theology*, Lonergan writes, 'Note that the word, critical, has two quite different meanings. In pre-critical history it means that one has tested the credibility of one's authorities before believing them. In critical history it means that one has shifted data from one field of relevance to another. On this topic, R.G. Collingwood is brilliant and convincing.'

RD

53

Bernard Lonergan Archives,
Lonergan Research Institute

Bernard J. F. Lonergan.
Insight: A Study of Human Understanding. Toronto: Published for the Lonergan Research Institute of Regis College, Toronto, by University of Toronto Press, 1992.

Although Lonergan finished writing *Insight* in 1953, the book was not published until 1957. The original publisher was Longmans, Green & Co., Ltd., of London. In 1958 a revised edition was published by the same publisher and by the Philosophical Library of New York. The North American rights were eventually transferred to Harper and Row, and now belong to the Bernard Lonergan Estate, which has issued the critical edition of *Insight* as volume 3 of the *Collected Works of Bernard Lonergan* published by the University of Toronto Press. The editorial notes reveal that the editors, Frederick E. Crowe and Robert M. Doran, found 130 discrepancies between Lonergan's original typescripts and the original published text. Some of these are incidental but several are very important (e.g., 'fraction' instead of Lonergan's 'function'). The *Collected Works* edition is as close to a critical edition of this monumental work as is possible.

RD

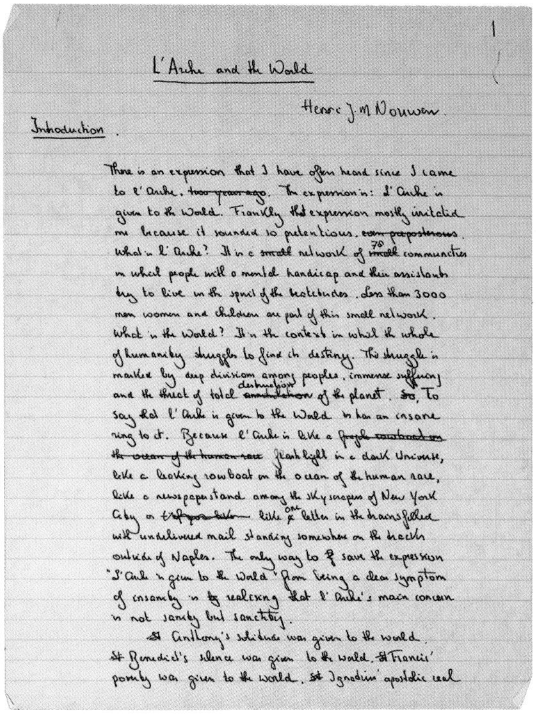

1

L'Arche and the World

Henri J.M Nouwen.

Introduction.

There is an expression that I have often heard since I came to l'Arche, ~~two years ago~~. The expression is: L'Arche is given to the World. Frankly that expression mostly irritated me because it sounded so pretentious. ~~even preposterous~~. What is l'Arche? It is a ~~small~~ network of 70 ~~small~~ communities in which people with a mental handicap and their assistants try to live in the spirit of the beatitudes. Less than 3000 men women and children are part of this small network. What is the World? It is the context in which the whole of humanity struggles to find its destiny. This struggle is marked by deep divisions among peoples, immense suffering and the threat of total ~~annihilation~~ destruction of the planet. ~~So~~, To say that l'Arche is given to the World has an insane ring to it. Because l'Arche is like a ~~fragile rowboat on the ocean of the human race~~ flashlight in a dark Universe, like a leaking rowboat on the ocean of the human race, like a newspaperstand among the skyscrapers of New York City or ~~[illegible]~~ like one letter in the drawers filled with undelivered mail standing somewhere on the tracks outside of Naples. The only way to save the expression "L'Arche is given to the World" from being a clear symptom of insanity is by realising that l'Arche's main concern is not sanity but sanctity.

St Anthony's solitude was given to the world. St Benedict's silence was given to the world. St Francis' poverty was given to the world. St Ignatius' apostolic zeal

54 Henri J. M. Nouwen (1932–1996)
'L'Arche and the World'. Manuscript. [1987?]

John M. Kelly Library, St. Michael's College

55 *Henri Nouwen meeting Pope John Paul II.* Arturo Mari, L'Osservatore Romano. Citta' Del Vaticano. Servizio Fotografico. [1987].

Henri J.M. Nouwen, author of more than forty books on the spiritual life, including *The Return of the Prodigal Son: A Story of a Homecoming* (1992), *The Genesee Diary* (1976) and *The Wounded Healer* (1974), was born in Holland in 1932, and ordained a Catholic priest in 1957. He spent most of his career in the United States teaching, first, in the Psychology Department at Notre Dame University, and later in the theology schools of Yale and Harvard. His classes were hugely popular, with students being drawn to them by his central themes of compassion, hospitality, contemplation, and community. Always seeking new ways to express and live his faith, Nouwen was involved with a variety of different groups and movements, including the American Social Justice Movement for Nuclear Disarmament, the Catholic Worker, liberation theology, and AIDS ministry, to name just a few. In 1986 he resigned from Harvard, to serve as spiritual minister to L'Arche Daybreak in Richmond Hill, Ontario, described by its founder, Jean Vanier, as 'communities where people whatever their race, culture, abilities or disabilities, can find a place and reveal their gifts to the world.' Nouwen continued to write, and to lecture widely, until his untimely death in 1996 of a heart attack while visiting Holland.

'L'Arche and the World' was written by Nouwen for a talk he gave at a Federation of L'Arche in Rome, Italy, in 1987. The manuscript draft is an example of Nouwen's writing style and method of composition, his earliest drafts emerging after periods of meditation almost complete in their development and scope, usually following a three-part structure. His writing tended to reveal his deeply personal reflections on universal themes, making the personal universal and the universal personal. Subsequent drafts of this paper are in the Archives and Research Collection along with manuscript and typescript drafts for his published and unpublished work, page proofs and galleys, and correspondence with publishers and his wide circle of friends who read drafts for comment.

The photograph shown here was taken by the official Vatican photographer during an audience with Pope John Paul II that was arranged for members of L'Arche during their annual meeting in 1987. Nouwen is in the centre shaking hands with Pope John Paul II. To the left of the Pope is Jean Vanier, founder of L'Arche, to the right is Andre de Juar, SJ. It is a rare photograph of Nouwen wearing the clerical collar. Although his dedication to the priesthood and the Catholic Church never wavered, Nouwen consciously avoided Church politics and preferred simplicity of expression over pomp and circumstance.   *GE*

MUSIC

56

Faculty of Music Library

Luis Milán (ca. 1500-aft. 1560)

Libro de mvsica de vihuela de mano. Intitulado El maestro. Valencia: Francisco Diaz, 1535.

This first printed collection of music for the vihuela (the Spanish member of the lute family) contains fantasias, pavans and villancicos. In the songs, the vocal melody in the tablature is in red, produced by double impression from movable type. Systems of tablature notation, which use one symbol to show how to produce the required sound, and another to show its duration, are still used for virtually all plucked-string music up to the present. As its title advertises, the book is a tutor in the reading of tablature, and the selection and tuning of strings. The pieces are arranged in increasing difficulty, with instructions for performance, as 'a teacher would do with a student who had never played.' It was composed during Milán's residence at the court of Germaine de Foix. A woodcut with the text 'Great Orpheus, creator of the vihuela,' appears between the introduction and the music. Milán describes himself as a second Orpheus, and there are references to his musical ability in contemporary Spanish poems. The Library's copy is one of only a handful extant, and the only complete one in North America. It was acquired from a New York dealer in 1970.

KM

57

Faculty of Music Library

Girolamo Frescobaldi (1583–1643)

Toccate d'intavolatvra di cimbalo et organo. Partite di diverse arie e corrente, balletti, ciaccone, passachagli. Libro primo-secondo. Rome: Nicolò Borbone, 1637.

Frescobaldi worked in Rome and Mantua as a keyboard virtuoso, teacher and celebrated composer. These books are his final revisions of collections originally published in 1615 and 1627. His music, with its evocation of intense and continually shifting feelings, is graphically complemented by the flowing and elegant appearance on the page. The printer, Nicolò Borboni was a successor to Simone Verovio, the calligrapher and engraver, who in 1586 had first adapted the process of printing from engraved copper plates to full-scale music production.

KM

58

Faculty of Music Library

Georg Frideric Handel (1685–1759)

Acis and Galate: a Mask as it was Originally Compos'd, with the Overture, Recitativo's, Songs, Duets & Choruses, for Voices and Instruments. London: I. Walsh, 1743.

Handel composed and probably performed this masque, or pastoral opera, to words by John Gay, for the Duke of Chandos at his Cannons estate in the summer of 1718. The first public performance was at Lincoln's Inn Theatre in 1731, and Handel made revisions up until 1739, including self-borrowings from a cantata written in 1708 in Italy on the same topic, *Aci, Galatea e Polifemo*. By 1700 large-scale commercial music engraving had been established in London by John Walsh the elder, who replaced the use of copper plates with less costly pewter ones, and introduced punches for some of the musical signs. The firm specialized in 'Favourite song' selections and had earlier issued several collections of excerpts, before this edition of the complete work. His son and successor fully developed the firm's relationship with Handel, publishing almost all his later works and in 1739 they were granted a monopoly of his music. This copy is one of many scores originally in the collection of H.H. Langton, the University's chief librarian from 1892 to 1923. He and his wife, Ethel Street, a founder of the Women's Musical Club of Toronto, were passionate amateur musicians. Music in print insists on being performed, rather than just 'read', and the observable vigorous usage of this score is not unusual.   *KM*

59
Faculty of Music Library

Baldassare Galuppi, called Il Buranello (1706–1785)
Il mondo alla roversa, o sia, Le donne che comandano; dramma giocoso per musica. …
Accommodato per il clavicembalo dal originale venetiano. Leipzig: J.G.I. Breitkopf, 1758.

Galuppi was one of the most significant composers of '*dramma giocoso,*' a term used for a type of libretto written by Carlo Goldoni and his followers, in which character-types from serious opera appeared along-side the peasants, servants, elderly buffoons and others traditional to comic opera. This work was his only opera published in full during his lifetime. In the mid 1750s Johann Gottlob Immanuel Breitkopf of Leipzig had made inventions and improvements in divisible and movable types, which made the publication of larger and more attractive editions possible. Virtually all notable composers of the second half of the eighteenth century attempted to have at least a few works printed or published by his firm. Now as Breitkopf & Härtel, after surviving World War II bombing, and post-war division in the two Germanies, it remains one of the foremost music publishers of the twenty-first century.   *KM*

60
Faculty of Music Library

Baldassare Galuppi, called Il Buranello
The Favourite Songs in the Opera call'd Il filosofo di campagna. London: I. Walsh, [1761].

Il filosofo di campagna, the most famous of Galuppi's nearly ninety operas, was produced first in Venice in 1754. It was successful all over Italy, was given at Frankfurt, Dresden and Prague in 1755, in Barcelona and St. Petersburg in 1758, and reached London in 1761, with the soprano Maria Angiola Paganini: her arias are featured in these excerpts with keyboard accompaniment for domestic use. Walsh, the enterprising printer and publisher, was also the first to adopt regularly the *passé-partout* technique of printing music title-pages. This involved the creation of generic plates – advertising similar publications in this case, using an elaborate illustration in others – with a blank area within which title information could be printed from a second, small plate or written in manuscript.   *KM*

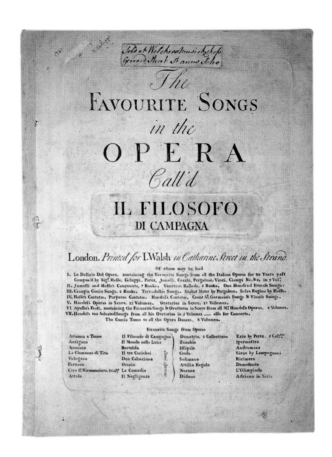

61
Faculty of Music Library

Christoph Willibald Gluck (1714–1787)
Alceste. Manuscript. Italy, ca. 1770.

62

Christoph Willibald Gluck
Alceste. Paris, ca. 1777.

Collections at Fisher and Music offer opportunities to examine aesthetic, social, and economic aspects of the dissemination of opera through manuscripts, libretti, full and piano-vocal scores, and stage guides (*mises en scènes*), and the differences in the purposes and uses of these formats. Beginning in the early eighteenth century, one can trace the gradual transformation of the public sphere for the performance and appreciation of music from one dominated by court and state to one that included an independent bourgeoisie. The Italian *Alceste,* first produced at the Vienna Burgtheater in 1767, was written to promote the 'reform' principles of Gluck and his librettist Ranieri de' Calzabigi, to replace the complicated plots and florid style of *opera seria* with noble simplicity in the action and music. This manuscript version reflects local cuts and changes for a later production, probably in northern Italy. The printed full score shows the extensive alterations made for performance in Paris in 1776, to a new French version of the text, by

François du Roullet. Near the end of act 1, Alceste's resolution to die for her husband Admetus, is expressed in the Italian in a lengthy recitative, '*Ove son?*'; in the French, a much shorter recitative, '*Où suis-je*' is followed by a lament and refrain, a scene with the High Priest, and an expansive air of defiance, '*Divinités du Styx*'.

KM

63
Faculty of Music Library

Mark Burnham (1791–1864)
Colonial Harmonist. Being a Compilation of the Most Approved Tunes, Anthems, and Chants. With a Figured Bass for the Organ and Piano Forte. Designed for all Denominations of Christians. Port Hope, U. C., 1836.

The first edition of *Colonial Harmonist* in 1832 was the earliest tunebook published in Upper Canada. This manuscript for a second edition is a rare surviving example of a 'mock-up' for the printer. Perhaps because of the success of Davidson's denominationally-supported 1838 book, it never reached publication. As is usual for North American nineteenth-century books of sacred music, which circulated in small communities lacking musical instruction, it starts with an introductory section 'Rudiments to the art of singing'. 'Tune' here means the harmonized setting for three or four vocal parts of a hymn melody. The text of the first verse is underlaid in the air in the tenor part. Several tunes have been identified as original compositions by Burnham. Its recent discovery and acquisition from descendants of the compiler were featured in an article in *The Halcyon, The Newsletter of the Friends of the Thomas Fisher Rare Book Library*.

KM

64
Faculty of Music Library

Alexander Davidson (1794–1856)
Sacred Harmony: Consisting of a Variety of Tunes, Adapted to the Different Metres in the Wesleyan-Methodist Hymn Book; and a few Anthems and Favourite Pieces; Selected from the most approved Authors, Ancient and Modern, under the Direction of the Conference of the Wesleyan-Methodist Church in Canada. … With a supplement. Toronto: Anson Green; J.H. Lawrence, 1845.

The combined University of Toronto Libraries have developed a significant collection for the study of North American psalmody, including most of the known nineteenth-century Canadian titles, and many American examples. *Sacred Harmony* was the most successful Canadian hymn tunebook, published in at least twelve editions from 1838 to 1861. This one is unique in its use of shape-notes, a system which originated in the mid-western and southern United States. A note head of a certain shape is assigned to each of the syllables fa, sol, la, mi. Singers with little musical expertise are enabled to sing at sight without having to recognize pitches on the staff or understand the key system. The musical repertoire reflects traditional favourites from the Reformation chorales and Psalters, adaptations of Handel and Beethoven in the English tradition, and some original tunes from American composers of the Revolutionary era, the 'Yankee tunesmiths.' Canadian place-names add a local flavour to many tunes.

KM

65

Ildebrando Pizzetti (1880–1968)

Assunta. Manuscript. Firenze, 1918.

This is a fair copy, in the composer's hand, of the second of *Due liriche drammatiche napoletane,* for high voice and piano, dedicated to 'Edoardi di Giovanni.' The songs were published in Florence in 1918 by Forlivesi. Edward Johnson (1878–1959), after whom the Faculty of Music building is named, was a Canadian tenor and impresario. He used this Italian adaptation of his name, Edoardi di Giovanni, during his studies and early operatic work in Florence, where he joined a circle of musical friends, including Toscanini. He performed leading roles in several premières, among them that of Ippolito in Pizzetti's first successful opera *Fedra*, with a libretto by Gabriel D'Annunzio, at La Scala in March 1915. He established himself after World War I as a leading singer at the Chicago Opera and later at the Metropolitan in New York, and finally as general manager of the Met from 1935–1950. The musical portion of his estate, held in the Faculty of Music, includes vocal scores with his markings, the sheet music of his recital repertoire, several composers' manuscripts such as this one, presentation copies of printed songs, photographs, programs, and his collection of medals and honours. *KM*

ARTS AND SCIENCE

Dodo.

TAB.XXVII

Pavo The Peacock.

Gallo pavo. The Turkey.

Gallina Africana.

66

ROM Library
Rare Book Collections

Francis Willughby (1635–1672) and John Ray (1627–1705)
Ornithologiæ libri tres. London: John Martyn, 1676.

One of the true gems of the J.H. Fleming Collection is Francis Willughby's and John Ray's *Ornithologiæ libri tres.* The naturalist Willughby and the botanist Ray met while students at Trinity College, Cambridge. Upon graduating they traveled together on natural history excursions through the northern counties of England and Wales. In 1663 they undertook a tour of continental Europe that lasted until 1665, when Willughby was summoned home to England by his father's death. He and Ray later continued their travels throughout southwest England. Willughby wanted to expand his travels with a trip to North America, but his plans were thwarted by ill-health which claimed his life at the early age of thirty-seven in July of 1672. Under the provisions of his will Ray was granted an annuity of £60. He tutored Willughby's three children, and eventually published Willughby's work *Ornithology,* first in Latin in 1676 and then in an enlarged edition in English in 1678. The original Latin edition held by the ROM is called 'the widow's edition' owing to the mention of Willughby's widow Emma on the title-page, along with the engraved vignette of the Willughby coat-of-arms. Emma had commissioned the seventy-seven illustrations for the work from the leading engravers of the day, including William Faithorne and William Sherwin. The metal engravings were a disappointment to Ray, who complained that he had not been able to supervise the engravers, thus leading to their misinterpretation of his ornithological instructions. Willughby's work is regarded as the 'foundation of scientific ornithology' (Alfred Newton, *Dictionary of Birds,* 1893–1896). Ray also edited Willughby's work on fishes and published *Historia piscium* in 1686. He also attempted to publish Willughby's work on insects, but died before its completion. It was eventually published by the Royal Society under the editorship of William Derham in 1710 as *Historia insectorum.* The leather-bound folio held by the ROM has undergone restoration of its binding. It bears the stamp of J.H. Fleming Zoological Library, Toronto, on the inside front cover and the title-page. Following the index are seventy-seven leaves of engravings. Inserted on the inside back cover is an envelope with newspaper clippings, bookseller advertisements and annotations by J.H. Fleming relating to Willughby and his books on ornithology.   *AS*

67

ROM Library
Rare Book Collections

Johann Bartholomew Adam Beringer (1667–1740).
Lithographiæ Wirceburgensis. Würzburg: P.W. Fuggart, 1726.

The Royal Ontario Museum of Palaeontology was one of the five founding museums that formed the ROM in 1914. Representing this subject area in the exhibition is the original 1726 Latin version of Beringer's *Lithographiæ Wirceburgensis.* This folio work is recognized as one of the first scientific hoaxes. Beringer was a senior professor at the University of Würzburg in Germany with a fascination for fossils. In 1725 some

'fossils' were recovered from a hill near Würzburg and delivered to Beringer. They were unique samples that intrigued him, and led him to believe he had uncovered new scientific findings. He combined his extensive research with finely engraved plates in his treatise published the following year. Shortly thereafter, Beringer is reported to have unearthed a stone inscribed with his name, and realized he had been duped. He attempted to buy back and destroy all the copies of his book, but was not entirely successful. In the judicial proceedings that ensued, the perpetrators of the hoax were identified as Professor J. Ignatz Roderick and Librarian Georg von Eckhart, colleagues of Beringer's at the University. Upon his death the copies he had acquired were discovered in his house. A publisher bought them and re-issued them in 1767 as a second edition with a new title-page. The account of Beringer's disgrace has been romanticized and embellished over the centuries. In 1963 the University of California Press published an English version, translated and annotated by Melvin Jahn and Daniel Woolf, entitled *The Lying Stones of Dr. Johann Bartholomew Adam Beringer.* The ROM's copy bears the bookplate of Frédéric Fauth, 'Docteur en médécine'. The book is bound in leather with gilt spine title and decoration. There are twenty-one numbered engraved plates illustrating the 'fossils' with such shapes as fanciful birds, beetles, butterflies, shellfish, plants, copulating frogs, moons and stars. An engraved frontispiece portrays a romanticized mound setting for the location of the fossils outside Würzburg, topped off by an obelisk. The ROM's copy is made even rarer by the inclusion of Georg Hueber's nine-page 'Reverendissime et celsissime princeps …' which precedes Beringer's text.   *AS*

68

ROM Library
Rare Book Collections

Francis Grose (ca. 1731–1791)

A Treatise on Ancient Armour and Weapons. London: Printed for S. Hooper, 1786.

The European collections of the ROM resonate in the memories of many museum visitors as they fondly recall the former armour court. Representing this subject interest in the exhibition is Francis Grose's *Treatise on Ancient Armour and Weapons.* It is illustrated with plates based on the original armour in the Tower of London, as well as other English collections such as that of Sir Ashton Lever. Born in London, Grose served as a foot soldier in Flanders, and later as a cornet in the dragoons. He left the military in 1751 to pursue his interest in sketching, taking lessons at William Shipley's drawing school in London. He returned to military life in 1759, but continued to engage in his artistic pursuits. He was a member of the Society of British Artists and exhibited at the Royal Academy. His first set of etchings appeared in the second edition of his brother John Henry Grose's *Voyage to the East Indies* published in 1766. Grose later wrote *The Antiquities of England & Wales* (1773–1776), *The Antiquities of Ireland* (1791–1795), *The Antiquities of Scotland* (1789–1791), and *A Classical Dictionary of the Vulgar Tongue* (3rd ed. 1796), all of which can be found in the William Barrett Collection at the Thomas Fisher Rare Book Library. The engraved frontispiece illustrates a fifteenth-century embossed steel shield, inlayed with gold, showing Scipio receiving the keys of Carthage. At the time of publication the shield was in the possession of Gustavus Brander of Christchurch, Hants., having been originally acquired in Italy by a Dr. Ward for £500. The volume also has an engraved title-page vignette in addition to forty-eight numbered engraved plates signed by John Hamilton, who was then serving as vice-president of the Society of British Artists. The leather-bound volume has gilt borders, spine decoration, and spine title, with a restored binding and new lining papers.   A S

69

John W. Graham Library,
Trinity College

Joseph Priestley (1733–1804)

Experiments and Observations on Different Kinds of Air, and Other Branches of Natural Philosophy, Connected with the Subject … abridged and methodized, with many Additions. Birmingham: Printed by Thomas Pearson, 1790.

A theologian and man of science, a radical in both politics and religion, Joseph Priestley wrote on many topics, none more important than this work, for which he is credited with the discovery of oxygen (which he called 'dephlogisticated air') and, hence, deemed the 'father of modern chemistry'. This abridgement of Priestley's seminal work was part of the personal library of John Strachan, first Bishop of Toronto and founder of both the University of Toronto and the University of Trinity College. Strachan made two substantial gifts to the Trinity College Library, the first comprising six hundred books in 1853, shortly after the founding of the College, the second a bequest of his three thousand volume library on his death in December 1867. Strachan's lifelong dedication to education, from his youthful years as a schoolmaster

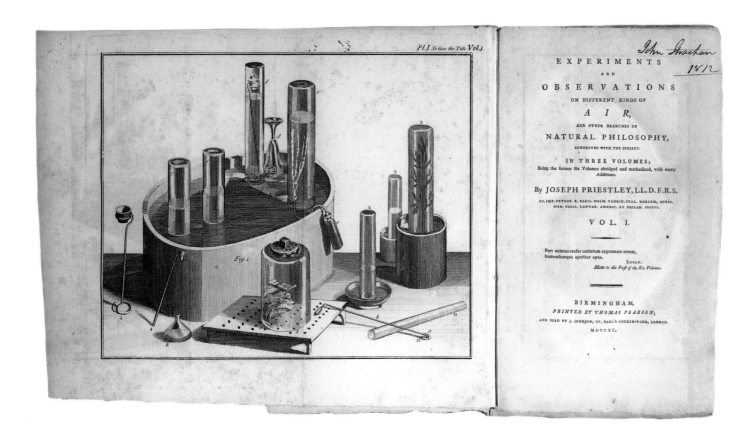

lured to Upper Canada in 1799 by the promise of advancement in this vocation, to his lasting involvement in the life of Trinity College, is reflected in the range of subjects his books covered: science, mathematics, classics, English literature, history, economics, politics and philosophy, as well as theology and doctrine, including orthodox Anglican thought, dissenting ideas, and controversial literature, as might be expected from the library of an eminent Anglican bishop. For a century or longer these books remained in the circulating collection of the Trinity Library. The wear and tear from scholars' use and challenging environmental conditions are evident in the physical state of many surviving volumes. Though its original paper boards and spine are frail, this three-volume work, with unopened pages and elegant engraved plates, remains substantially in excellent condition. It bears the original Strachan gift bookplate from 1853 and his signature dated 1812 on the title page.

LC

70

ROM Library
Rare Book Collections

Ottavio Bertotti Scamozzi (1719–1790)
Le terme dei Romani disegnate da Andrea Palladio. Vicenza: Giovanni Rossi, 1797.

Architecture and design are a major research interests of curators at the ROM. The rare book collections were greatly strengthened in this subject area by the substantial donation of the Robert Baldwin Fordyre Barr Collection, represented in this exhibition by Ottavio Scamozzi's *Le terme dei Romani disegnate da Andrea*

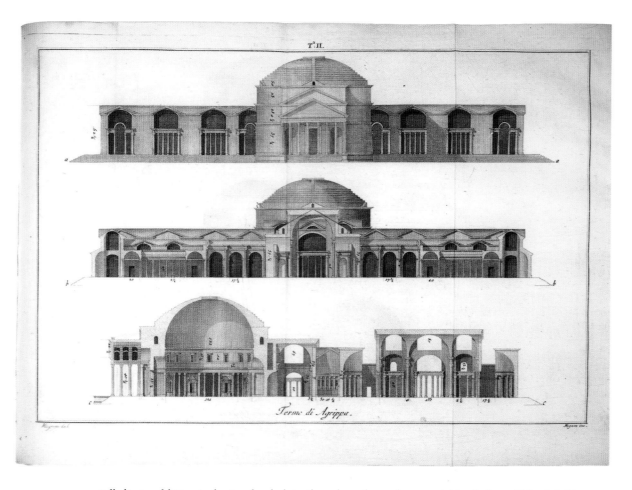

Terme di Agrippa.

Palladio. In addition to the Barr bookplate, the volume bears the armorial bookplate of John L. Pakington. The marbled calf leather bindings have gilt cover fillets and spine decoration. The title and numbering are gold-stamped on red spine labels. The volume was bound as number five in a set of Scamozzi's works, with the first four volumes being volumes one to four of his *Le fabbriche e I disegni di Andrea Palladio* (1796). This rare Italian text is accompanied by twenty-five numbered engraved plates of which sixteen are folded. The engraved frontispiece features an engraving of a bust of Andrea Palladio attributed to Richard Boyle, Lord Burlington, who promoted the Palladian style of architecture throughout England.

Scamozzi was born Ottavio Bertotti in 1719, but later added Scamozzi to his name in recognition of a legacy he received from the estate of Vincenzo Scamozzi. The legacy was designated for a promising young student of architecture with the condition that the recipient adopt the Scamozzi name. Vincenzo had completed three of Andrea Palladio's buildings and incorporated Palladian features into his own architectural designs. Ottavio published a guide to Palladian Venice in 1761 (also held by the ROM) under the title *Il forestiere istruito della cose piu rare di architettura e di alcune pitture della citta di Vicenza*, with its focus on Renaissance architecture and devoted to buildings designed by Palladio and Vincenzo Scamozzi. Over the course of his career Ottavio completed over thirty architectural works, primarily restorations and reconstructions in and around Venice.

AS

FIG.19

UNDRESS.

London Published as the Act directs Oct.r 1803 by Madam Lanchester. N.o 17 New Bond Street

71

ROM Library

Rare Book Collections

The Miroir de la mode. London: Madame Lanchester. Volume 1 (1803).

In support of the extensive textiles and costume collections of the ROM, the Rare Book Collections house an excellent collection of early periodicals featuring fashion plates. One of the earliest titles held by the ROM is *The Miroir de la mode*, a monthly that began publication in 1803. It is believed to have survived for a brief period until 1804. The ROM's holdings comprise a single bound volume for 1803. It is illustrated throughout with hand-tinted engravings. Very little is known about Madame Lanchester beyond the fact that she was a prominent London modiste in the early nineteenth century with a showroom on New

Bond Street. Her fashion plates appeared in many of the fashionable ladies' journals of her day, including Rudolph Ackermann's *Repository of Arts and La Belle Assemblée*. The ROM's volume of *The Miroir de la mode* comes from the William Barrett Collection. This Collection had been assembled by the Dublin barrister Quintin Dick during the late eighteenth century and the first half of the nineteenth century. Upon his death in 1858 his estate passed to his nephew William Hoare Hume, and later to William Henry Barrett of Port Dover, Ontario. The collection was donated by the Barrett family to the ROM in 1984. In 1997 the bulk of the Barrett Collection was transferred to the Thomas Fisher Rare Book Library, with the ROM retaining titles that pertained to the museum's collections.

AS

72

Thomas Fisher
Rare Book Library
- OISE Collection

William Combe (1742–1823)
A History of the University of Oxford, its Colleges, Halls, and Public Buildings. London: Printed for R. Ackermann, by L. Harrison and J.C. Leigh, 1814.

Combe is described in the *Dictionary of National Biography* as both a 'writer and literary imitator'. Although a man of independent means in his youth, towards the end of the eighteenth century he experienced a series of financial embarrassments that saw him intermittently confined to a debtors' prison. In his latter years his income was largely dependent on his relationship with the publisher of this two-volume set,

Rudolph Ackermann (1764–1834), who was also an art dealer. Early in the nineteenth century Combe began to write the letterpress for a series of illustrated histories, among which is the present title. The two volumes contain 114 hand-coloured plates (including aquatint and stipple engravings) drawn and engraved by some of the finest illustrators of the day, notably Augustus Charles Pugin (father of the great architect), Frederick Mackenzie, and William Westall. This remarkable two-volume set was rebound by Zaehnsdorf, the great London firm established in 1842. They form part of the collection transferred by the Ontario Institute for Studies in Education to the Fisher Library in 2003.   *PJC*

73	George Baxter (1804–1867)
Victoria University Library	*Her Most Gracious Majesty Queen Victoria Receiving the Sacrament at her Coronation.* London, 1841.

74   George Baxter

Her Most Gracious Majesty Queen Victoria Receiving the Sacrament at her Coronation. London, 1841. (printed in sepia)

75   George Baxter

The Great Exhibition (Interior). London, 1851.

76   George Baxter

The Great Exhibition (Interior). London, 1851. (proof pull)

In 1835, lithographer and engraver George Baxter patented an innovative method to produce colour prints in quantity from blocks and plates using oil-based inks. His aim was to imitate oil painting and provide good, inexpensive art that mirrored the taste and sentiment of the early Victorian period. The Baxter process began with the engraving of a scene onto a metal plate in lines of varying strength to obtain gradations of light and shade. Relief wood blocks, superimposed over each other, were used to apply colours in order to complete the print. Pictures were built up slowly, tint by tint, a process that depended upon exacting standards of registration in the printing. Often prints were then touched up by hand resulting in a rich thick colour print with a glossy surface. Baxter provided colour printed illustrations for eighty-seven books, but eventually concentrated on the production of individual prints like those included here.

At the coronation of Queen Victoria on 28 June 1838, Baxter was accorded special facilities in the gallery occupied by the Foreign Ambassadors in Westminster Abbey to sketch the event for a commemorative print. The scene includes about two hundred portraits of the various dignitaries present at the coronation. The work entailed in producing the colour prints was considerable and completed prints did not appear until 1841. The delay meant a financial loss for Baxter, one of many he would incur. Although Baxter was able to renew his patent in 1849, he was advised to sell licenses to former apprentices and others who wished to use the process. The Great Exhibition of 1851 provided an opportunity for Baxter to demonstrate his skill in a series of commemorative prints. In addition to views of the exterior and interior, including the print shown here in two versions, he produced a number of smaller prints of the art work displayed at the Exhibition. Baxter continued to work through the 1850s, but faced increasing competition in the field of colour printing and eventually relinquished his business. He died bankrupt in 1867.

The Starr Collection of Baxter Prints and Illustrated Books was presented to Victoria University Library in 1945 by Anne Callander MacKay Starr in memory of her husband Frederic Newton Gisborne Starr – a graduate of Victoria's medical program and member of the Board of Regents from 1915 until his death in 1934. The collection includes many examples of Baxter licensees, among them prints and illustrated books by Le Blond & Company and Kronheim. GZ

77

Robertson Davies Library,
Massey College

John Weale (1791–1862)

Divers Works of Early Masters in Christian Decoration … With Examples of Ancient Painted and Stained Glass, from York, West Wickham, Kent, and St. George's Chapel, Windsor; … also a succinct Account, with Illustrations, of Painted and Stained Glass at Gouda, in Holland, and The Church of St. Jacques at Liège. London: John Weale, 1846.

From humble beginnings as an errand boy for a London bookseller, John Weale established his reputation as a bookseller, publisher, and writer in the field of architecture. He worked initially with George Priestley and later Priestley's widow, Mary, who took Weale into partnership about 1819. Under the name of Priestley & Weale, he began publishing architectural books, a specialty he greatly expanded in 1834 when he acquired the business of Isaac Taylor and continued under the firm name of 'John Weale'. Weale was much involved in the writing and editing of the works he published. He also took great care in the accuracy of the reproductions, both of the architectural detail and the colours. For this book, he employed the architect and pioneer in chromolithography, Owen Jones (1809–1874), to supervise the printing of the chromolithographic plates. The work was highly praised and earned Weale a gold medal from the King of Belgium in 1847. The two-volume set, along with other works by Weale, came to Massey College when the Ruari McLean Collection of Victorian Book Design and Colour Printing was purchased in 1970.   *MK*

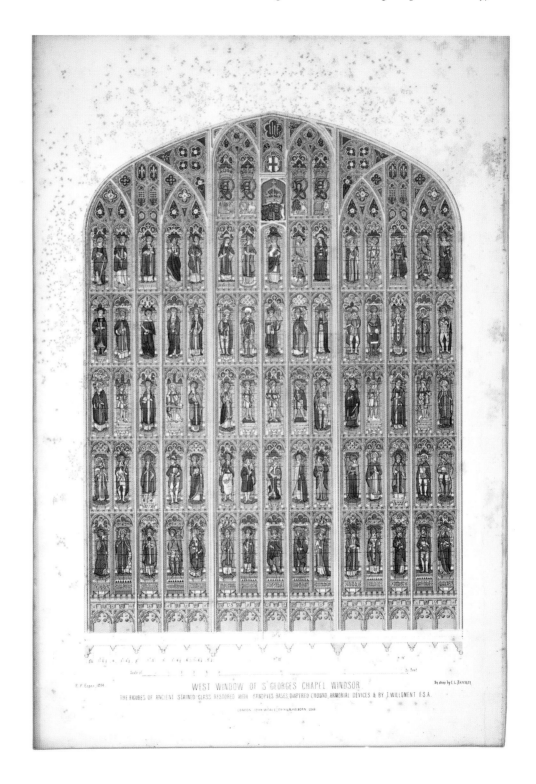

WEST WINDOW OF S.º GEORGES CHAPEL WINDSOR.
THE FIGURES OF ANCIENT STAINED GLASS RESTORED WITH CANOPIES BASES, DIAPERED GROUND, ARMORIAL DEVICES & BY J. WILLEMENT. F.S.A.

78

Robertson Davies Library,
Massey College

Agnes Miller Parker (1895–1980)
Proofs of a wood engraving of 'The Frogs and Jupiter' for the Gregynog Press edition of
The Fables of Esope. [Newtown, Wales, 1931].

The Gregynog Press was founded in 1922 as part of a cultural centre established by Gwendoline and Margaret Davies at the great country house of Gregynog near Newtown, Wales. The aim of the press was to encourage fine book production in Wales and all aspects of a Gregynog Press book – design, typesetting, presswork, illustrations, and bindings – were carried out at the manor. Between October 1930 and September 1933, four artists were associated with the press: Blair Hughes-Stanton (1902–1981) and his wife, Gertrude Hermes (1901–1983), and William McCance (1894–1970) and his wife, Alice Miller Parker, with McCance handling the administrative role of 'controller'. It was a productive, yet tumultous period with conflicts between the artists and the Board of Directors who oversaw the press, and personal difficulties between Hughes-Stanton and Hermes. When McCance returned to his native Scotland, he retained a personal archive of Gregynog Press material which included trial copies and proofs of initial letters, page layouts, and the wood engraved illustrations, as well as the final version of the books and ephemera produced during his tenure. These proofs are part of that archive which was acquired by Massey College in the early 1970s.

MK

79

Thomas Fisher
Rare Book Library
- Hart House Collection

The Holy Bible. Oxford: At the University Press, 1953.

Popularly known as the 'Coronation Bible', this book, printed under the direction of Charles Batey, Printer to the University of Oxford, forms part of the Hart House Collection at the Thomas Fisher Rare Book Library. Among its many distinguishing characteristics is the fact that the book was the work of a single compositor. While the vast majority of these Bibles were printed on regular paper, an additional twenty-five were printed on Oxford India paper, of which Fisher's copy is number seventeen. The choice of India paper for the limited edition was not merely aesthetic but was linked to the logistics of the ceremony itself. Standard issue paper, it was believed, would have made the book too bulky to be used gracefully, while the light India paper would be more easily manoeuvred. Fisher's copy belonged to Vincent Massey, eighteenth Governor-General of Canada who represented the nation at the Coronation. (The Queen took her Oath on copy number one.) The book is most memorable, however, for its striking binding. It was designed by the accomplished engraver and artist, Lynton Lamb (1907–1977), who studied bookbinding under Douglas Cockerell and was charged with the task of redesigning the bindings for the OUP's Bibles and prayer books. In preparing the design of the Bible, Lamb was concerned that decoration should follow structure. He wrote that 'if one has taken a great deal of care over sewing the sheets to the cords, rounding the back, and making the boards true, one does not want to break down these effects by a contrary scheme of decoration. In this instance, the design of interlacing lines springs from the six cords on which the sheets are sewn; and while the gold lines are turned this way and that to catch the light, their pattern and that of the crowns and ciphers in blind and gold tooling powdered over the ground empha-sizes the flatness and rectangularity of the boards.' The choice of a red-coloured binding was also made so that the book would blend in with the splendour of the other regalia. It boasts a scarlet levant goatskin cover on which Lamb imposed a large cream-coloured lozenge with the royal cipher, E II R, surmounted by a crown, in the centre. The intention was to attract the eye with a striking contrast, given that the book would be the focus of attention at one of the most pivotal moments in the liturgy. The actual binding was executed by Sangorski and Sutcliffe.   *PJC*

HISTORY AND TRAVEL

80

ROM Library
Rare Book Collections

George Sandys (1578–1644)
Sandys Travels, Containing an History of the Original and Present State of the Turkish Empire.
London: John Williams Junior, 1673.

The founder of the ROM, Charles Trick Currelly, was an avid collector of books as well as classical antiquities. His copy of *Sandys Travels* by Sir George Sandys bears his bookplate, as well as that of the Hon. Marmaduke Dawnay. The signature of the famous British portrait painter Sir Joshua Reynolds is found on the leaf following the end of the text. Sandys traveled to the Levant via France, Italy and Constantinople in 1610, and spent a year in Turkey, Palestine and Egypt. His observations were first published in 1615 under the title: *A Relation of a Journey Begun An. Dom. 1610*. The ROM's folio copy is the seventh edition, and bears the engraved title page for the sixth edition dated 1670. It is illustrated with fifty engraved maps and illustrations, including one folded plate and one folded engraved map. It also includes numerous decorative woodcut vignettes, and is bound in light brown leather, with gilt decoration embossed on the spine and borders. The title in gold is embossed on the spine. The text is notable for one of the first references to coffee and was regarded as the authoritative text on the Levant for its day. Sandys went on to become treasurer for the colony of Virginia from 1621 until 1625. He was appointed the colony's agent in London in 1639, and served in that capacity until his death in 1644.

AS

Cornelis de Bruyn (1652–1726 or 27)

Voyages de Corneille Le Brun par la Moscovie, en Perse, et aux Indes Orientales. Amsterdam: Frères Wetstein, 1718.

This title from the ROM's collections takes us farther east to Russia, Persia and India with the voyages of the Dutch painter Cornelis de Bruyn. The original account of his travels was published in *Reizen over Moskovie, door Perzie en Indie* in 1711. De Bruyn was born in 1652 in The Hague, and took painting lessons with Theodoor van Schuer. He left the Netherlands for Rome in 1674, where he became known as Adonis. He was a member of the *Shildersbent*, a social organization of Dutch and Flemish painters in Rome known for their Bacchic celebrations. In 1701 he traveled to Persia and India via Moscow, arriving in Persia in 1703. He spent three months drawing the ruins at Persepolis, where his signature remains visible to this day in one of the monuments of the Archæmenid Palace. De Bruyn's profusely illustrated volumes document the social customs he witnessed, as well as the antiquities, flora and fauna of the region. His work was met with considerable criticism by his contemporaries, for his engravings of Persepolis varied from those of other travel books of the period. However, later scholarship vindicated him, regarding his drawings and descriptions as accurate depictions of the period. The French edition of this work contains an engraved portrait of De Bruyn, and large folded panoramic views of 'Moskow' and 'Spahan'. This two-volume set was bound in leather with gold embossed borders and spine decoration, and was labelled as *Voyages de Le Brun*. The same binding was applied to the author's 1714 work *Voyage au Levant*, and labelled as vol. III.   *AS*

Page 507.

Grand Maître de l'Ordre
de Constantin

82

ROM Library
Rare Book Collections

Honoré de Saint Marie (1651–1729)
Dissertations historiques et critiques sur la chevalerie ancienne et moderne, séculière et régulière.
Paris: Pierre-François Giffart, 1718.

The medieval period of European history is well represented in the ROM's collections, and for this exhibition we have selected this work by Father Honoré de Saint Marie, also known by the secular name of Blaise Vauxelle. The ROM has the original 1718 edition, while the 1729 edition is held by the Thomas Fisher Rare Book Library. The ROM's copy is bound in vellum, and includes twelve leaves of engraved plates illustrating the emblems of the orders of knighthood and chivalry. The illustration selected for the exhibition shows the Grand Master dressed in the regalia of the Order of Constantine, a Byzantine order of knighthood for priests and laymen dating back to 1191.

AS

83

John W. Graham Library,
Trinity College

Charles Cordiner (1746?–1794)
Original watercolour drawings for *Antiquities & Scenery of the North of Scotland, in a Series of Letters to Thomas Pennant.* London; 1780, and *Remarkable Ruins, and Romantic Prospects of North Britain, with Ancient Monuments, and Singular Subjects of Natural History.* London: 1788–1795.

These seventy-seven original watercolour drawings by the Reverend Charles Cordiner (Episcopal minister of St. Andrew's Chapel, Banff, Scotland) were the basis for engravings by Peter Mazell which were first issued in parts with Cordiner's descriptive text and subsequently re-ordered and collected in printed volumes. A superb example of a genre popularized earlier by naturalist and traveller Thomas Pennant (1726–1798) in his Scottish tours (1769 and 1772), Cordiner's work is a valuable source for the study of the natural and built environments and the cultural sensibility – notably, Romanticism – of eighteenth-century Scotland, as expressed by a gifted clergyman trained at the Foulis Academy of Art in Glasgow. Cordiner died at the age of forty-eight before the last part was published, leaving a widow and eight children, for whom the proceeds from this publishing venture would have been of material importance. In addition to this volume of watercolour drawings, another volume contains annotated proof copies of the engravings in the earlier work, bound with seven original drawings and Cordiner's accompanying printed series of descriptive letters to Pennant, ostensibly in response to Pennant's specific entreaty. This unique four-volume set, uniformly bound in red morocco gilt by J. Bowtell, Cambridge, bears bookplates indicating that it was at one time owned by the antiquary, R.M. Trench Chiswell (1735–1797) and later by noted collector J.R. Abbey (1896–1969), before it was acquired in 1964 by J. Kemp Waldie, Toronto bookman and proprietor of the Golden Dog Press from 1933-39. Gift of Guy and Sandra Upjohn in 1995.   *LC*

84

Robertson Davies Library, Massey College

Statistical Chart of the Great Exhibition Showing at a View the Number and Class of Visitors on each Day, and the Receipts at the Doors. Presented to the Purchasers of the Weekly Dispatch, May 16, 1852. London: Printed in Colours at Vizetelly & Company's Offices ... and Published by R.J. Wood, at the 'Weekly Dispatch' Office, 1852.

On 1 May 1851 Queen Victoria opened the Great Exhibition of the Works of Industry of All Nations in London. The international exposition had been two years in the making, organized by a Royal

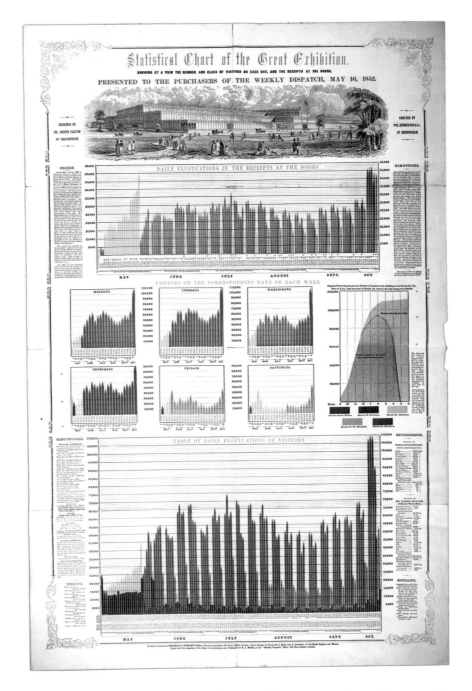

Commission over which Prince Albert (1819–1861) presided. It featured fourteen thousand exhibitors from seventy-seven countries showing the best of their arts and manufactures. The display was housed in the Crystal Palace, a marvelous structure of glass and iron devised by Joseph Paxton (1801–1865) and erected in the southeast end of Hyde Park. Over six million visitors came during the six and a half months the Great Exhibition was open. Ticket prices ranged from season tickets at £3. 3s., good for admission at any time, to one shilling tickets, issued after 22 May and valid only Mondays to Thursdays. Between the sale of tickets and refreshments, the Great Exhibition generated a revenue of £505,107 5s. 7d., almost a third of which was surplus to its expenses. The fluctuations of visitors and receipts at the door, along with other statistics, are graphically illustrated in this keepsake. A marvel of colour printing, it was acquired in 2003 to complement other material on the Great Exhibition in the McLean Collection of Victorian Book Design and Colour Printing.

MK

85

Robertson Davies Library,
Massey College

George Cruikshank (1792–1878)
London, in 1851 [and] *Manchester, in 1851.* London: David Bogue, 1851.

The Great Exhibition drew visitors from all over the world, but especially from all parts of Britain as people took advantage of special excursion rates on the railways or packaged tours organized by workingmen's associations. The fate of these visitors to London was humorously depicted by Henry Mayhew (1812–1887) and George Cruikshank in *1851: or The Adventures of Mr. and Mrs. Sandboys and Family, Who Came Up To London To 'Enjoy Themselves,' and to See the Great Exhibition.* The ten plates by Cruikshank also were sold separately at fifteen shillings per set. Copies of both, along with guidebooks, catalogues of the contents of the Great Exhibition, and other material on the subject, are part of the McLean Collection of Victorian Book Design and Colour Printing.

MK

86

Edward S. Curtis (1868–1952)
The North American Indian. Seattle: E.S. Curtis, 1907–1930.

The *crème de la crème* of the ROM's Rare Book Collections is the complete set of Edward Curtis' *The North American Indian*, published by Curtis in a limited edition of five hundred sets between 1907 and 1930. The Curtis's ROM's copy is number 22, a gift from Curtis' patron, J. Pierpont Morgan, who had been a financial backer for C.T. Currelly's Egyptian expeditions noted earlier in this text. The set includes twenty text volumes with 1510 illustrations, and twenty portfolios with 723 plates. The illustrations are published photogravure images documenting the traditional customs and traditions of eighty Native American tribes encompassing the Great Plains, Great Basin, Plateau Region, Southwest, California, Pacific Northwest, and Alaska. Curtis undertook his first photography expedition in 1900 with a visit to the Blackfoot Indians in Montana to photograph the sun dance. He formally began work on *The North American Indian* project in 1901, with the anticipation of completion within five years. In 1906 Curtis gained the backing of President Theodore Roosevelt, who wrote a foreword to the text. Roosevelt introduced Curtis to J. P. Morgan, who offered Curtis $75,000 in support of his project. In return Morgan received twenty-five sets and five hundred original prints. The first volume was completed the following year in 1907. By the time the project was completed, Morgan and his son Jack had contributed grants amounting to over half of the $1,500,000 final cost of the project. Two Curtis photographs were selected for the exhibition from the set of portfolios. 'On The Canadian River' is plate number 659 from volume nineteen, showing a party of Cheyenne riders on the banks of the Canadian, which originally divided the lands of the Quapaw to the south from those of the Great and Little Osage to the north. The name of the river is unrelated to Canada, but rather comes from the Spanish cañada, referring to the high, cut banks of the stream. 'Carved Posts at Alert Bay' is plate number 330 from volume ten. It shows two heraldic columns at a Nimkish village on Cormorant Island. They represent the owner's paternal crest, and eagle, and his maternal crest, a grizzly bear crushing the head of a rival chief.

AS

87

Great Britain. Army of the Rhine
Special Edition. The Cologne Post. A Daily Paper published by the Army of the Rhine. Cologne, Thursday, May 8 1919. The Draft Treaty of Peace 'For the Prevention of Wars in the Future and for the Betterment of Mankind'. Cologne: Printed and published by 'The Cologne Post' May 7, 1919.

This is a remarkable survival of the original moulds used to create the stereotype plates for printing a newspaper. Briefly, the stages of production were as follows: the text would be set in type which was proof-read and corrected, if necessary; the type was then covered with flong (alternate layers of blotting paper and tissue paper) which was beaten onto the type to create a mould or matrix; metal was poured into the mould to create a stereotype plate which was then used for printing. In this instance, the four moulds are for the pages of a special issue of *The Cologne Post* which announced the terms of the Treaty of Versailles. The text was summarized under the following headings: 'Descriptive Introduction to summary'; 'Preamble'; 'Section I. The League of Nations'; 'Section II. Boundaries of Germany'; 'Section III. Political clauses of Europe'; 'Section IV. Political clauses outside of Europe'; 'Section V. Military, naval, and air clauses'; 'Section VI. Prisoners of War'; 'Section VII. Responsibilities for the crimes of the war'; 'Section VIII. Reparation and restitution'; 'Section IX. Finance'; 'Section X. Economic clauses'; 'Section XI. Aerial navigation'; 'Section XII. Ports, waterways and railways'; 'Section XIII. The labour convention'; 'Section XIV. Guarantees'; and 'Section XV. Miscellaneous' provisions. *The Cologne Post* was the official newspaper for the Army of the Rhine, published daily from 31 March 1919 to 17 January 1926, and continued as *The Cologne Post and Wiesbaden Times* from 28 January 1926 to 3 November 1929. The occupying forces left Germany in December 1929. It was hard to resist such a wonderful and rare example of printing technology when it was offered for sale in an English antiquarian bookseller's catalogue in 2004. It is now part of the bibliography collection at Massey College.   *MK*

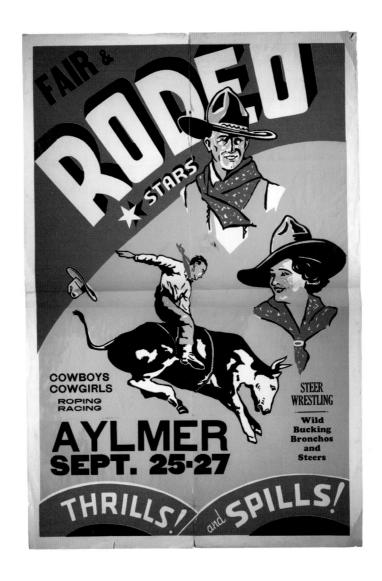

Fair & Rodeo Stars. Cowboys Cowgirls Roping Racing Steer Wrestling Wild Bucking Broncos and Steers. Aylmer Sept. 25-27 Thrills! And Spills! [Rouleau, Saskatchewan: Enterprise Show Print, between 1923 and 1940].

By 1914 the railway connected most parts of Canada, bringing travelling circuses, carnivals, and theatrical companies to places like Rouleau, Saskatchewan. A small community fifty kilometres southeast of Regina, Rouleau had two daily express trains linking it with the main line of the Canadian Pacific Railway. It also was home to a pioneering printer and publisher, Andrew King (1885–1981), who had moved there from Manitoba to establish the *Rouleau Enterprise*, a weekly newspaper, in 1909. Three years later, a chance encounter with an agent for a Chicago theatrical group, desperately in need of advertising posters, led King to expand his business to include show prints. At first he used wood type of different sizes and styles to produce the posters. In 1914 he introduced a pictorial element, using large woodblocks, one for each of the primary colours (yellow, red, and blue), which he engraved by hand. The paper changed over the years, with the early posters being printed on a thin paper, while a heavier card called 'box board' was used from about 1940 to 1958. Within a few years, King's 'Enterprise Show Prints' was producing posters for companies throughout North America. When King moved to Estevan and purchased *The Estevan Mercury* in 1944, he continued the poster operation under the name 'King Show Prints' until 1958 when his newspaper business was acquired by a company based in England. Sometime in the late 1960s, Douglas Lochhead, then Librarian of Massey College, visited Andrew King in Estevan and came away with five woodblocks and several posters. The three blocks for this rodeo poster, cut in 1923, and two for a circus poster produced in 1934 now hang in the Bibliography Room at Massey College as an integral part of the teaching collection of the Massey College Press.

MK

89

John W. Graham Library,
Trinity College

Collection de tracts, brochures et journaux préparé par le Political Warfare Executive et Distribués en France et dans les Territoires Français. Londres, 1940–1944.

This collection of some 250 leaflets produced for distribution by air over France during World War II to encourage the Resistance Movement contains speeches or excerpts of speeches by Churchill, Roosevelt, Eisenhower, and others, translated into French. The accompanying 'secret' letter from Churchill's secretary R.E.K. Hill to his publisher H. Aubrey Gentry, director of Cassell and Company, requests permission to reprint Churchill's speeches in a miniature booklet for similar dissemination as wartime propaganda. The 'specimen' issue of *La France Libre* (Octobre 1942) was included with the letter to indicate the quality of the proposed publication. A possible outcome of this initiative is the booklet *Discours de guerre de Winston Churchill 1940–1942,* printed by Shenval Press in March 1943 for a department of the Foreign Office for clandestine distribution in occupied France and French North Africa. Like many other items from the Graham Library's extensive collection of the works of Winston Churchill, this 'scrapbook' of leaflets in mint condition was owned by the prominent collector, H.A. Cahn, before it was acquired by F. Bartlett Watt, Toronto, and given by him to the Trinity College Library in 1995.

LC

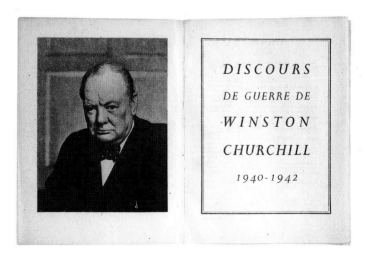

90

Renault Protests. Our immediate strike claims: 1.40-hour week at once without reduction in wages 2. 1,000 ƒ minimum wage 3. Old-age pension at 60, at 55 for women 4. A fifth week of paid holidays for the young workers 5. Revision of social security measures 6. Freedom for trade unions [Paris, 1968].

91

Support the students against the Establishment. [Paris, 1968].

May 1968 was a period of political upheaval in Paris. Student demonstrations led to worker sit-in strikes and to the widespread general strike that paralyzed the country and threatened the French political regime. This worker/student rebellion shut down most of France and eventually ended General De Gaulle's political career. The demand was for the reorganization of French social and political life. Barricades went up; street fighting broke out; and the Sorbonne was occupied by students and converted into a huge commune. During this time of political and social upheaval, the *École des Beaux Arts* was occupied by students who formed the *Atelier Populaire*: workshops where the posters were first conceived, then produced using silk-screening processes, lithography and stencilling. The *Atelier populaire* considered the posters they produced as weapons both in the service of their struggle and the workers' protest against the 'Establishment'. Victoria University Library owns nineteen posters donated by Professor Emeritus Paul Bouissac who was doing research in Paris in May, 1968. *GZ*

BELLES-LETTRES

A Song of Liberty

1. The Eternal Female groand! it was heard over all the Earth:

2. Albions coast is sick silent; the American meadows faint!

3. Shadows of Prophecy shiver along by the lakes and the rivers and mutter across the ocean? France rend down thy dungeon;

4. Golden Spain burst the barriers of old Rome;

5. Cast thy keys O Rome into the deep down falling, even to eternity down falling,

6. And weep and bow thy reverend locks!

7. In her trembling hands she took the new born terror howling:

8. On those infinite mountains of light now barr'd out by the atlantic sea, the new born fire stood before the starry king!

9. Flag'd with grey brow'd snows and thunderous visages the jealous wings wav'd over the deep.

10. The speary hand burned aloft, unbuckled was the shield, forth went the hand of jealousy among the flaming hair, and hurl'd the new born wonder thro' the starry night.

11. The fire, the fire, is falling!

12. Look up! look up! O citizen of London enlarge thy countenance: O Jew, leave counting gold! return to thy oil and wine; O African! black African! (go. winged thought widen his forehead.)

13. The fiery limbs, the flaming hair, shot like the sinking sun into the western sea.

14. Wak'd from his eternal sleep, the hoary element roaring fled away:

15. Down rush'd beating his wings in vain the jealous king; his grey brow'd councellors, thunderous warriors, curl'd veterans, among helms, and shields, and chariots horses, elephants: banners, castles, slings and rocks,

16. Falling, rushing, ruining! buried in the ruins, on Urthona's dens.

17. All night beneath the ruins, then their sullen flames faded emerge round the gloomy king,

18. With thunder and fire: leading his starry hosts thro' the waste wilderness

92   William Blake (1757–1827)

Marriage of Heaven and Hell, Copy M, *A Song of Liberty*, c. 1790.

93   William Blake

Songs of Innocence and Experience, Copy O, plate 39, 1831.

94   William Blake

Songs of Innocence and Experience, Electrotype, 1860.

William Blake, poet, artist, engraver, printer, visionary, and mystic developed a method of 'illuminated printing' for the production of his books. Using copperplates and relief-etching, Blake conceived of his work as a complete unit in which text and decoration form an integral design, and thus as writer, artist, and printer, he was able to control all aspects of their production. *Marriage of Heaven and Hell* consists of a compilation of satiric prose sketches directed at the religious visionary and prolific writer Emanuel Swedenborg and the Swedenborgian New Church whose General Conference Blake attended in 1789. Inspired by the French Revolution and the storming of the Bastille, Blake etched a two-leaf political pamphlet poem called *A Song of Liberty*. The three plates of *Song* normally occur as the last three plates of the *Marriage of Heaven and Hell*. Copy M is unusual in having the *Song* printed on one sheet forming four pages with the first page left blank. This suggests that perhaps Blake printed it this way to form a separate pamphlet. Copy M represents an important bibliographic discovery about Blake's illuminated printing: differing considerably from the one other known pamphlet-like copy, it provides insight into Blake's work as printmaker and printer, revealing much about his techniques and editing practices.

Blake invented his method of relief etching in 1788 and *Songs of Innocence* was among the first 'illuminated books' which he produced and published in this way. Etching is an intaglio process in which the design is produced by acid penetrating below the surface of a copper or steel plate, the surface itself being protected by an acid-resistant varnish. Blake reversed this process, drawing and writing directly on the plate with an acid-resistant varnish, and etching the background away, which left the image and text as a relief or raised surface. With the assistance of his wife Catherine, plates printed in monochrome were coloured by hand using a transparent watercolour wash.

Copy O, plate 39 of *Songs of Innocence and Experience* was printed posthumously from Blake's original copperplate in 1831. Electrotypes were made from the copperplates in about 1860 for use in Alexander Gilchrist's *Life of William Blake: Pictor Ignotus,* (London: Macmillan, 1863). The original plates were lost by Frederick Tatham who had taken possession of them after the death of Catherine Blake. Before the Gilchrist electrotypes were destroyed by the publisher in 1961 copies were made for the Fitzwilliam

Museum and for Geoffrey Keynes, Blake bibliographer and editor; the example displayed is from a set made by the Fitzwilliam Museum for G.E. Bentley Jr. in 1964.

The G.E. Bentley Jr. Collection of approximately 2,500 works by and about William Blake and his contemporaries came to Victoria University Library in 2005. A product of more than fifty years of scholarly book and print collecting and often the source for Bentley's many bibliographical and biographical publications, the collection includes original Blake manuscripts and prints, Blake's contemporary commercial engravings plus modern reproductions and facsimiles, the manuscripts and drawings of Blake's close friend George Cumberland, books by John Flaxman, illustrated books before 1835, and Blake scholarship and criticism.   *RCB*

95 Samuel Taylor Coleridge (1772–1834)
Victoria University Library   Christabel. Holograph Manuscript. Feb-Apr 1798; August-October 1800.

96 Samuel Taylor Coleridge
Christabel: Kubla Khan, a Vision; The Pains of Sleep. London: Printed for John Murray, 1816.

The *Christabel* manuscript and the first printed edition of the poem are part of Victoria University Library's Samuel Taylor Coleridge collection. The research collection which includes manuscripts, letters, books from Coleridge's library, and transcripts by members of Coleridge's family and circle including Wordsworth, Southey and Lamb, was acquired from the Coleridge family through the efforts of Professor Kathleen Coburn, general editor of *The Collected Works of S.T. Coleridge*, an editorial project based at Victoria College (1969–2002).

Kathleen Coburn was invited to meet Lord Geoffrey and Lady Coleridge at the family home in Ottery St. Mary Devon, in 1930. Coburn, a Victoria College, University of Toronto graduate had recently arrived in England, and had just embarked on her postgraduate studies at Oxford University. At this time, Samuel Taylor Coleridge's library and papers were held by two branches of the Coleridge family: the direct descendants of Samuel Taylor Coleridge and the descendants of Coleridge's brother James. The Ottery St. Mary collection of manuscripts was extensive and contained the notebooks of the 1818–1819 Philosophical Lectures that Coburn edited and published in 1949. That collection was purchased in the 1950s by the British Museum.

Victoria University Library's Samuel Taylor Coleridge collection was purchased on behalf of Victoria University by Kathleen Coburn in 1954 from the poet's great, great grandson – A.H.B. Coleridge. The collection reflects the family's editorial project. Following S.T. Coleridge's death, Sara Coleridge and her husband Henry Nelson Coleridge, and subsequently Derwent Coleridge and his son Ernest Hartley Coleridge, undertook the task of systematically editing and publishing Coleridge's poetry, philosophical essays, literary criticism, lectures, and conversation.

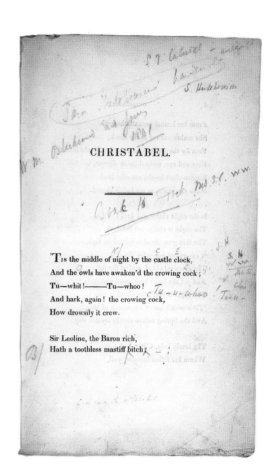

Christabel was written in two parts; Part I in 1798 while Coleridge was working on *The Rime of the Ancient Mariner*; and Part II in 1800 following Coleridge's travels in Germany. Manuscript copies of *Christabel* circulated widely to family and friends, and the poem was also recited by Coleridge and members of his circle to sympathetic listeners. Byron was very taken with the poem. He gave Coleridge £100 to finance its publication, and arranged for his publisher John Murray to print the poem together with a fragment from *Kubla Khan* and *The Pains of Sleep* (a poem that tells of nightmares induced through opium addiction). Three editions of *Christabel* were published between May and June 1816.

This manuscript of *Christabel* was copied by the poet in either 1800 or 1801 and presented to Sara Hutchinson – Coleridge's muse, amanuensis, and sister-in-law of his close friend, the poet William Wordsworth. Pasted into the notebook (likely at a later date), also in the poet's hand, is the sonnet *To Asra*. This is the only extant holograph of *To Asra*. A facsimile of the *Christabel* manuscript was produced in 1907 by the Royal Society of Literature. It was the first Coleridge manuscript to be published in photographic facsimile. E.H. Coleridge's markings in this first edition copy of the poem reflect the complexity of editing the *Christabel* text. The annotations 'WW' and 'MS EC' seen on these pages refer to two manuscripts of Christabel: the 'Wordsworth manuscript' which was written partly in Coleridge's hand and partly in Mary Hutchinson's hand (Mary Hutchinson was the wife of William Wordsworth); and the second, the Edith Coleridge manuscript seen in this exhibition.   *AG*

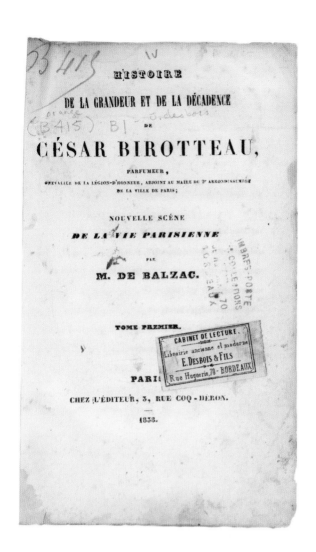

97

Honoré de Balzac (1799–1850)

Histoire de la grandeur et de la décadence de César Birotteau, parfumeur, chevalier de la Légion d'honneur, adjoint au maire du 2e arrondissement de la ville de Paris. Paris: Chez l'éditeur [Boulé], 1838.

Balzac started thinking about *César Birotteau* as early as 1831, but the novel was completed only a few days before its actual publication by Boulé in mid-December 1837. It was offered as a gift to subscribers of *Le Figaro*, which belonged to Boulé and was typeset in great haste, from 17 November to 15 December 1837. Only the first edition (shown here) includes an article that appeared in *Le Figaro* on 15 December, relating the absolute despair of the compositors and proofreaders, as Balzac sent to the printing shop page after page of barely legible copy. Bearing witness to the pace of the work, both volumes contain substantial *Errata* lists.

This particular copy of *César Birotteau* is one of the remnants of a nineteenth-century Bordeaux circulating library, the *'Cabinet de lecture E. Desbois'*, bought in 1996 by the Kelly Library for the Centre for 19th Century French Studies. The circulating library first belonged to Jean-Baptiste Magen, who ran it from 1817 to 1862. It was then sold to Pierre-Augustin Desbois, whose daughter, Emma, was to take over the business in 1872. Madame Desbois added stamps and rare books to her commerce and it thrived. Over the years, she more or less abandoned the circulating library and concentrated her attention on rare books, building an excellent reputation for her collection. The *Librairie ancienne et moderne,* as her circulating library came to be known, was still in operation in 1940.

YP

98

Robertson Davies Library, Massey College

William Makepeace Thackeray (1811–1863)

Mrs. Perkins's Ball. London: Chapman & Hall; Vizetelly Brothers and Co., Printers and Engravers, [1847].

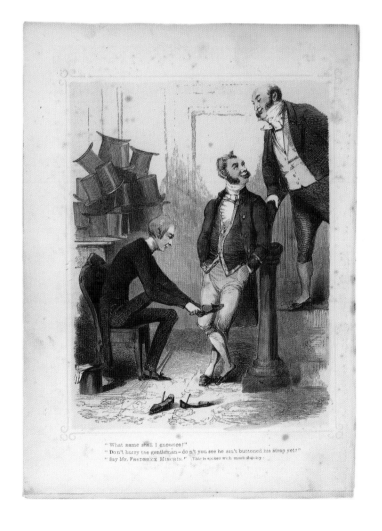

"What name shall I enounce!"
"Don't hurry the gentleman—do n't you see he ain't buttoned his strap yet?"
"Say Mr. Frederick Minchin." This is spoken with much dignity.

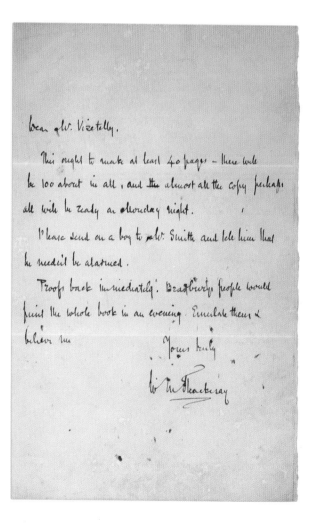

99

William Makepeace Thackeray
Autograph letter signed to Mr. [Henry] Vizetelly (1820–1894), [London, 1850?].

In the years that he was establishing himself as a writer, William Makepeace Thackeray frequently had dealings with James Vizetelly (1817–1897) and his brother, Henry, whose firm was known for its decorative printing and engraving. Thackeray contributed essays to accompany illustrations by Joseph Kenny Meadows (1790–1874) for *Heads of the People* (1840-41), which was printed by James Vizetelly. When Henry established *The Pictorial Times* in 1843 as a rival to the *Illustrated London News*, Thackeray served briefly as art critic and literary reviewer. The firm of Vizetelly Brothers and Co. printed the first and some of the subsequent editions of Thackeray's *Notes of A Journey from Cornhill to Grand Cairo* (1846), as well as the first two of his Christmas books, *Mrs. Perkins's Ball* (1847) and *Our Street* (1848), all of which were published by Chapman & Hall. Henry Vizetelly also produced many of the engravings after Thackeray's drawings which illustrated these works. When the partnership between the two brothers ended in 1849, Thackeray continued his relationship with both. The letter shown here probably was sent to Henry as he printed *The Kickleburys on the Rhine* for Smith, Elder & Co. The copy of *Mrs. Perkins's Ball* in its original decorative glazed paper boards was once part of the library of Anne and Fernand G. Renier. It was purchased in 2003, while the letter was acquired in 2005. Both items were added to the McLean Collection of Victorian Book Design and Colour Printing which contains much of the decorative printing done by the Vizetellys.   *MK*

100

John M. Kelly Library,
St. Michael's College

Émile Zola (1840–1902)
Autograph letter signed to Charles O'Neill Conroy. Médan, near Paris, 22 June 1890.

Zola's somewhat cryptic message – that he will give no explanation and that he believes his books speak for themselves – is a reply to a letter written a few days earlier by Charles O'Neill Conroy, in his capacity as secretary of the Italian Literary Society of Powis Square, London, England. In his letter, Conroy communicates to Zola the Society's decision to ban the reading of Zola's novels, which were highly controversial in late-Victorian England, unless Zola provided the members with a statement of his arguments in favour of Naturalist literature. Zola's curt reply put an end to the exchange of correspondence. The young Conroy (who was nineteen at the time he wrote the letter) would later immigrate to Newfoundland, to begin his career as a lawyer in St. John's. In 1913, he received his Q.C., and, the following year, was named Chief Notary of the Newfoundland Supreme Court. His contributions during the First World War to the legal organization of the Newfoundland Regiment earned Conroy the Order of the British Empire. In 1920, he was named Attorney General for the Maritimes and Newfoundland. The letter was a gift from the Montreal Conroys to the Centre for 19th Century French Studies at St. Michael's College. It is part of an extensive collection of books, microfilms, iconography, and manuscripts that constitute the Émile Zola Archives.   *DES*

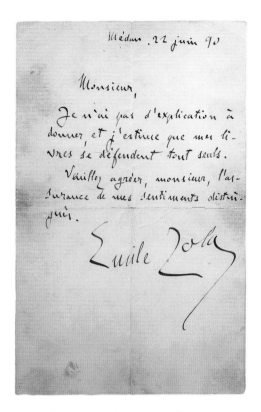

101

G.K. Chesterton (1874–1936)

[*Sketch book*]. ca. 1895.

102   G.K. Chesterton

Greybeards at Play: Literature and Art for Old Gentlemen. London: R. Brimley Johnson, 1900.

Although G.K. Chesterton is known primarily for his literary output, his parents originally intended him to be an artist. In 1892 (at the age of eighteen) he was sent to the Slade School of Art in London, where he spent three years studying art theory and technique, but also attending other lectures at the University of London. Several dozen sketchbooks survive from Chesterton's time at the Slade. Most are now in the British Library; the Kelly Library owns two, in addition to a number of individual sketches. Most of Chesterton's artistic work is comprised of cartoons and doodles – but done with such excellence that he is often able to capture the personality of his subjects. Many of these cartoons are of malevolent characters or of people holding weapons. Describing his time at the Slade, Chesterton wrote, 'There is something truly menacing in the thought of how quickly I could imagine the maddest, when I had never committed the mildest crime.' Even after determining that his skills were more literary than artistic, Chesterton continued to sketch. He did the illustrations for several of his own books, and had drawings published in a number of magazines. He was also responsible for the illustrations for a dozen books by his close friend Hilaire Belloc, the last of which was published in 1936, the year of his death.

As a young man G.K. Chesterton had a number of individual poems and book reviews published in several literary magazines. *Greybeards* was his first published book. A collection of poems and sketches, it is arranged in three series: 'The Oneness of the Philosopher with Nature', 'Of the Dangers Attending Altruism on the High Seas', and 'On the Disastrous Spread of Aestheticism in All Classes'. The lofty-sounding titles are somewhat deceptive, since the book is actually a work of satire. Although the work was favourably received by critics, Chesterton himself seems not to have taken great pride in it and did not mention it in his *Autobiography*. Some years later he commented, 'To publish a book of my nonsense verse seems to me exactly like summoning the whole of the people of Kensington to see me smoke cigarettes.' The copy of *Greybeards* displayed here was originally given by the author's uncle Arthur Chesterton to one of his friends.

NM

103

Victoria University Library

Virginia Woolf (1882–1941)
Mrs. Dalloway
London: Published by Leonard and Virginia Woolf at the Hogarth Press, 1925.

104

Vanessa Bell (1879–1961)
Design for the dust jacket of *Mrs. Dalloway*. Graphite, ink and watercolour, 1925.

Vanessa Bell and her sister Virginia Woolf were daughters of the biographer Leslie Stephen and central members of the Bloomsbury group of artists, writers, and intellectuals that flourished in the early twentieth century. Virginia married Leonard Woolf in 1912, pursuing a career as a novelist, essayist, biographer, and critic. Many of her works questioned the traditional role of women in society, but also dealt with broader issues such as the difficulties of personal relationships, the precariousness of the human condition, and the inadequacies of language itself. To express this, she developed a stream-of-consciousness 'modernism', allowing the reader to see characters through multiple points of view. She solidified this style in *Mrs. Dalloway*, which was her fourth novel. The book took two years to write and only two thousand copies of this first edition were published. The reviews were generally positive and the book sold well, becoming one of her best-known and admired works, whose influence has continued in books, movies, and even musical compositions.

Vanessa studied briefly at the Slade School of Art, Pelham School of Art, and Royal Academy Schools. She married the art critic Clive Bell in 1907. As an artist she worked in many media and, in addition to painting, she designed fabrics, ceramics, stage sets, and interiors. She was a co-director with Roger Fry of the Omega Workshops from 1913 to 1919 and had four of her works displayed in the Post-Impressionist exhibition of 1912. Vanessa created the distinctive wolf's head logo for the Hogarth Press and designed a number of dust jackets for her sister's books, including *Jacob's Room, To the Lighthouse, A Room of One's Own, The Waves, The Years, Three Guineas,* and others. Their strong aesthetic appeal 'used to speak to us across a crowded bookshop'. Her dust jacket designs were of a limited palette, usually black and white with one other colour, and were intended to relate to the subject-matter of the book. In the case of *Mrs. Dalloway,* the black and white contrasts anticipate the emotional complexities of the novel with its themes of life and death, sanity and insanity, exhilaration and fear, and the artistic style reflects the impressionist narration. The flowers in the foreground represent the ones that the main character in the novel sets out to purchase as her day begins. Thus, in comparing the final dust jacket with the design, it is interesting to note that the candlesticks on

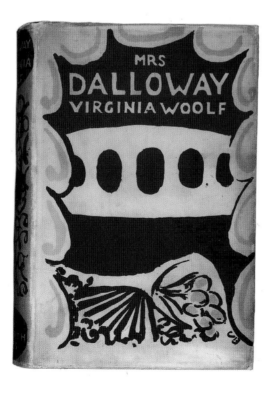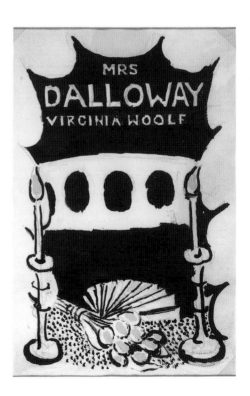

either side have been removed, the fan is now pointing downwards, and the detailed, textured style is replaced with broader, more abstract strokes.

The Virginia Woolf/Hogarth Press/Bloomsbury collection at Victoria University Library was founded on the first editions donated by Mary Coyne Rowell Jackman. The collection has grown and now numbers over 3700 items, including all the books hand-printed by the Woolfs, a nearly comprehensive collection of the Hogarth Press machine-printed books, as well as variant bindings, issues, proofs, signed copies, limited editions, translations, and ephemeral publications. In addition, original sketches and dust jacket designs enhance the research utility of the collection, bringing together the literary, visual creativity and decorative arts which characterized Bloomsbury.   *CKS*

105
Victoria University Library

Northrop Frye (1912–1991)
Notebook 7. Notes for *Anatomy of Criticism* and diagrams (1948).

106

Northrop Frye
Early notes for *Anatomy of Criticism* written on a printed notice for a luncheon honouring Lester B. Pearson on the occasion of his installation as Chancellor of Victoria University, 1952.

Throughout his *Anatomy* notebooks, Northrop Frye sketched out the mandala, a symbolic circular figure with symmetrical divisions often used in Buddhism and other religions as a representation of the universe. The circle or mandala is the core of *Anatomy* divided into two hemispheres, the top half representing the epic and the bottom, fiction. For Frye, the mandala symbolized his vision of the cosmology or the totality of literature.

After having drafted out his work through diagrams and tables in his early notebooks, *Anatomy of Criticism* became more formalized as a series of lectures given by Northrop Frye in 1954 after his appointment as Class of 1932 Visiting Lecturer at Princeton University. The book is an expansion of the four public lectures delivered at that university in March 1954. Upon publication by Princeton University Press in 1957, *Anatomy* initially garnered few reviews. It has since become one of the most quoted academic books of its time.

During the time leading up to the publication of *Anatomy*, Frye sketched mandalas as well as a number of complicated tables he used to categorize the forms that literature could take. In his diaries, Frye often chastised himself for his laziness with regard to his writing and thinking, but the fact that he spent part of the luncheon honouring Pearson working on a table to formulate ideas that would become central to his work, suggests a mind that was seldom disengaged from it.   *LS*

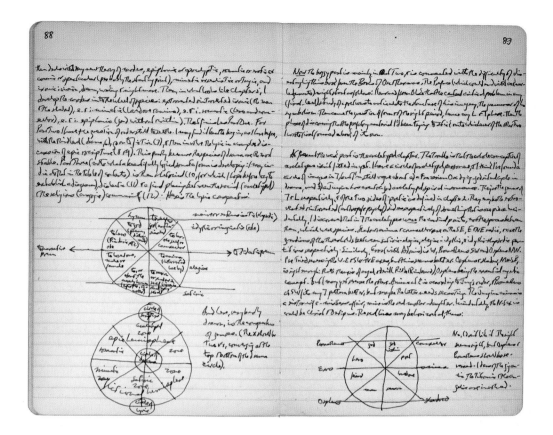

107
Victoria University Library

William Blake (1757–1827)
The Complete Writings of William Blake, with all the Variant Readings, edited by Geoffrey Keynes. London: Nonesuch Press, 1957.

This copy was owned and annotated by Northop Frye. Early in his career, Frye immersed himself in the writings of William Blake and prided himself on his knowledge of the poet's work. 'I know Blake as no man has ever known him' he wrote to Helen Kemp in 1935. In 1947, Princeton University Press published Frye's seminal study of William Blake, *Fearful Symmetry*, a product of fifteen years of research and still in print. Northrop Frye entered Victoria College as an undergraduate in 1929. He left Toronto to attend Merton College, Oxford where he received an MA in 1940, but otherwise Frye spent his academic career as a Professor of English at Victoria College. He became an internationally recognized scholar and lectured at universities throughout the world. At Victoria he divided his time between teaching, writing, and administration, serving as Principal of the College (1959–1967) and as Victoria's Chancellor (1978–1991). The greater part of the Northrop Frye papers was given to the Victoria University Library by Frye himself at irregular intervals from 1978 to 1990. After his death in 1991, there were further accruals of correspondence, manuscripts, photographs, essays, articles, notebooks, and other literary files, as well as his personal library of more than two thousand books with annotations such as this book.   *LS*

108
*Thomas Fisher
Rare Book Library
– University College Collection*

Irving Layton (1912–2006)
In the midst of my fever. [s.l.]: Divers Press of Palma de Mallorca, 1954.

109

Margaret Atwood (1939–)
Double Persephone. Toronto: Hawkshead Press, 1961.

University College has had a library since its founding in 1851. Indeed the University Library was housed there when the catastrophic fire of 1890 destroyed it, as a result of which we are unable to display a copy of the Audubon elephant folio in this exhibition. In 1893 the first separate library was completed and the special collections, such as they were and based primarily on the donations from North America, Great Britain, and Europe to replace the book stock, went there.

   In 1990, Avie Bennett, an alumnus of University College, purchased the literary portion of the collection of the poet Al Purdy and donated it to his *alma mater*. Most of it remains there, but a few of the rare presentation copies of works by iconic Canadian writers were transferred on deposit to the Fisher Library. The two featured here bear the following inscriptions: 'For my friend, Al, with admiration for his wonderful poems and appreciation for his continuing friendship. Irving Layton' and 'For Al – hope you understand it – I don't anymore – Best, Peggy 1970'.

RL

110

John M. Kelly Library,
St. Michael's College

Marshall McLuhan (1911–1980)
Distant Early Warning Deck. [Toronto:] 1969.

Marshall McLuhan remains arguably Canada's most famous intellectual. A convert to Catholicism, McLuhan was actively involved in life at St. Michael's College, where he taught from 1946 to 1979. In *Understanding Media* (1964) McLuhan wrote: 'I think of art, at its most significant, as a DEW line, a Distant Early Warning system that can always be relied on to tell the old culture what is beginning to happen to it.' Built during the Cold War, the DEW Line was an integrated chain of radar and communication stations designed to provide advance warning to Canada and the United States of imminent air attack. The McLuhan Dew-line was published in twenty issues in various formats including newsletters, posters, and even a deck of cards, between July 1968 and October 1970. This is part of the St. Michael's Publications Collection, one which brings together many of the works written by members of the St. Michael's faculty, staff and student body, past and present – including such notables as Marshall McLuhan and Morley Callaghan.   JB